And if a stranger sojourn with thee in your land, ye shall not vex him. But the stranger that dwelleth with you shall be unto you as one born among you, and thou shalt love him as thyself; for ye were strangers in the land of Egypt . . .

LEVITICUS, XIX: 33-34

Love thy neighbor as thyself.

LEVITICUS, XIX: 18
and MATTHEW, XIX: 19

The Puerto Ricans

CLARENCE SENIOR, a native of Missouri, since 1936 has specialized in the personal as well as economic and political relationships between the peoples of Latin America and ourselves. He has lived in various Latin American republics and in Puerto Rico. He has organized work camps in Mexico for the American Friends Service Committee, directed the Inter-American Institute of the University of Kansas City, and served in Brazil and Chile as consultant on immigration studies to the United Nations Economic Commission for Latin America. He was associate director of the Columbia University study of the Puerto Rican migrant in New York City and co-author of *The Puerto Rican Journey: New York's Newest Migrants.* While he was director of the Social Science Research Center of the University of Puerto Rico he became interested in and made several studies of Puerto Rican migration. He headed a study of Jamaican migration to Great Britain in 1955; the report was adopted by the Caribbean Regional Economic Committee as the basis for the organization of the West Indian Migration Services in the United Kingdom. He migrated from Puerto Rico to New York City in 1948. Currently, he is doing a study on migration and urbanization for the American Society of Planning Officials, and serving as a consultant to the Secretary of Labor of the Commonwealth of Puerto Rico. From 1950 to 1961, he taught at Columbia University, from which he holds a doctorate in sociology and economics. His book *Land Reform and Democracy* was published in 1958. He became Professor of Sociology at Brooklyn College, City University of New York in September, 1961, and in the same month was named a member of the New York City Board of Education.

The Puerto Ricans

STRANGERS—THEN NEIGHBORS

by Clarence Senior

FOREWORD BY HUBERT H. HUMPHREY

ILLUSTRATED
PUBLISHED IN COOPERATION WITH
THE ANTI-DEFAMATION LEAGUE OF B'NAI B'RITH BY

QUADRANGLE BOOKS *Chicago*

 For information, address: Quadrangle Books, Inc., 180 North Wacker Drive, Chicago 60606.

Manufactured in the United States of America.

Library of Congress Catalog Card Number: 65-18241

The Anti-Defamation League of B'nai B'rith wishes to express its gratitude to the Department of Education and the Information Office of the Commonwealth of Puerto Rico for permission to use the photographs in this book.

Second Printing

Foreword

I am pleased to recommend this excellent introduction to our Puerto Rican neighbors by Clarence Senior. Puerto Ricans come as the newest of the waves of migrants to our shores. They differ, however, in one major respect from the Irish, the Germans, the Italians, and all others who have preceded them: the Puerto Ricans come as American citizens. The United States obtained the island from Spain in 1898. U.S. citizenship was granted to the residents in 1917. Since 1948 they have elected their own governor and have developed a vigorous modern democracy, in which the natural capacities of Puerto Ricans for community building have flourished.

Mr. Senior has done a fine job of putting the Puerto Rican immigration in perspective. Unfortunately, many patterns of older waves of immigration to the United States have been repeated. The newcomer is a stranger. He has much to learn. He is not always accepted, and even when he is, problems of language, custom, and habit cause misfortune and error. One of the heartening things about Mr. Senior's book, however, is the evidence it provides of how much real progress has been made in assimilating and integrating Puerto Ricans into our society. This book dispels, with facts, many myths about Puerto Ricans, and as it is widely read it cannot help but facilitate a solution of the problems these people face when coming to the United States. While this is an optimistic and hopeful book, it does not gloss over the problems of education, housing, job discrimination, and general acceptance which so often confront the immigrant. We still have a job to do. Puerto Ricans are an industrious, responsible, ambitious people. They have much to add to the cultural pluralism which is the strength of America.

Mr. Senior concentrates on the Puerto Ricans who come to the United States. He has not, however, neglected their homeland which has a Commonwealth status as part of our country. This island has made such steady economic growth and progress that it is known as "the miracle of the Caribbean." Representatives from many of the underdeveloped countries of the world would come to Puerto Rico to study its model of progress.

This is an informative book and a needed one. Fresh meaning has been given to the epigraph which the author has chosen from the book of *Leviticus* in the Old Testament, urging that "the stranger that dwelleth with you shall be unto you as one born among you."

HUBERT H. HUMPHREY

Contents

Introduction

STRANGERS—THEN NEIGHBORS.

This has been the story of millions of us. From the beginning of American history, men and women from many lands have come to our shores who were, at first, strangers to one another. They became neighbors by working together, by facing endless problems cooperatively, by building communities, by uniting in civic, religious, labor, farm, and hundreds of other groups to work for their common good.

Thus, slowly and sometimes painfully, the great and powerful institution known as the United States of America has been built, starting with a handful of citizens and now counting over 190,000,000. Millions have come from foreign shores to make their homes here. They were strangers—they became neighbors. Every year millions of us move from one locality to another. We become strangers—then neighbors.

Generally, we are—as we have been in the past—a friendly, neighborly, hospitable people. We owe a large part of our strength to these qualities.

But—some of us have always been suspicious or afraid of newcomers. Now some of us are reacting with suspicion and fear again. Others of us are simply annoyed and irritated by a new stream of strangers flowing into New York, Chicago, Philadelphia, Bridgeport, Cleveland—into dozens of other urban centers. Some of these strangers are our fellow citizens from Puerto Rico.

We want to examine what is happening to them, and—just as important—to the rest of us. Let us first consider them against the background of what happened to millions of other strangers who came before them.

The Puerto Ricans

Chapter 1
OUR ANCESTORS AS BUILDERS

We know our ancestors came from all the lands of the earth. We know they cleared the forests, tilled the fertile lands, bridged the thousands of rivers, conquered the Appalachians and later the Rockies, spanned the Great Plains with bands of steel and then with concrete strips. Men and women of all creeds and colors, working together, tamed a continent.

The United States, from its inception to the present day, has been marked by the diversity of the sources of its population. New York City, especially, has been famous for its cosmopolitan character. Eighteen different languages were being spoken on Manhattan Island in 1644 when it was still part of the Dutch Empire.

The opening of new lands, the building of canals and railroads, the California Gold Rush and other spectacular metal and mineral developments, the building of a far-flung industrial structure, all required men and women in large numbers. Farms and factories multiplied and grew in size and production. The service trades in the cities then demanded more workers.

Steamship lines and then railroads created recruiting offices in towns and cities throughout Europe. The bigger industries followed suit, and the various states joined in the competition to find additional sources of manpower. The railroads also recruited in Asia; by the mid-eighteen hundreds, the Irish trackworkers of the East were matched by the coolies of the Western roads.

Meanwhile, Southern plantation owners had worked out their own system of recruitment in Africa which forcibly brought the ancestors of our more than 19,000,000 Negro fellow-citizens to the United States. They and other employers had for years followed another semi-forced labor system known as indenture, in which a man or woman bound him- or herself to work for a given term of years in exchange for passage money to the "New World."

Many of our ancestors were driven from their homes by religious or political persecution. Many others were forcibly evicted from their lands and in desperation became indentured servants. Still others were scooped up out of debtors' prisons or public almshouses and piled onto ships bound for America. But all of these involuntary immigrants were only a drop in the bucket compared to the mainstream.

The Economic Influence

Immigration was closely linked to the economic growth of our country. This is indicated not only by the letters and books which so many of our ancestors wrote but also by careful studies done by social scientists. These studies show, overwhelmingly, that immigration was extremely sensitive to the rise and fall in business activity. When workers were needed, they came; when recessions or depressions reduced job opportunities, immigration was reduced. The time lag between the opening up of economic opportunity and the arrival of the worker was about half a year, except in the case of immigation from Canada which reacted more quickly to changes in business conditions in the United States.

Lack of job opportunities quickly brought reductions in the movement to our shores; the major depressions of 1908 and 1930-40 showed net movements back to the country of origin.

There was always something of a return flow, however. Data for the years from July 1, 1907, to June 30, 1923, show that the volume of alien departures was equal to 51 per cent of the volume of alien arrivals. The ratio of departures to arrivals fluctuates greatly from year to year and from group to group. Italians arriving from the south of their country totaled about 1,500,000 in that period; those returning to their homeland totaled about 1,000,000, or around 66 per cent of the total. Northern Italians, while smaller in number, showed a ratio of 50 per cent. Greeks and Poles had almost as high a percentage of returnees, but Jewish re-migration was less than 10 per cent.

Great Britain, which had been a country of great emigration, received back 507,000 net during the years 1931-39.

The grand total of those who came to help each other build our country from 1776 to the middle of 1963 was 42,952,260. Six years in this century saw one million or more arrivals: 1905, 1906, 1907, 1910, 1913, and 1914.

There were always voices raised against immigration. Some felt that the inflow of people was once advantageous, but that "conditions have changed," as Representative Otis told Congress. "When the country was new it might have been a good policy to admit all. But it is no longer . . ." The gentleman from Massachusetts was addressing his colleagues in 1797.

Faster, Bigger, and Better

But our ancestors were builders. As they built, the land became capable of supporting more people—indeed, needed more people to help it build faster, bigger and better. The 3,022,387 square miles which composed the 48 mainland states supported, at a lower level of material well-being and physical comfort, some 900,000 Indians before the white man arrived. They now support over 200 times that many persons at the world's highest level of income.

Today we Americans own and drive more (and bigger) cars, talk over more telephones, listen to more radios, look at more television sets, bathe in more bathtubs, are better housed, clothed, and fed than any other nation in the world. We spend more money on education (and have a greater proportion of our people in school) than any other large nation. Churches, social services, hospitals and charities of all kinds are probably more widespread than in any other similar area, and there are millions spent on "the finer things of life" such as music, theater, and opera. There are few places in the world where civic participation through voluntary, non-governmental organizations is as widespread as in the United States.

Economically, "life chances" are good for the averge man and those who are above the average on the economic scale. However, there are many who do not "come up to the average." Almost one-third of all our families (31 per cent) had incomes in 1961 of less than $4,000. Thirteen per cent received even less than $2,000. We find that there are whole groups and whole regions in which many citizens are disadvantaged by poverty. Those who are poor live shorter lives, suffer from more diseases (both contagious and chronic), get fewer chances at education for themselves or for their children, and are more likely than the rest of us to be born, live and die in the same locality and even in the same occupation as their fathers.

One-Sixth of a Nation

Geographically, disadvantaged groups are found more in the South than in the North, but there are substantial "pockets" of such groups throughout the eroded-out farming areas of New England and the Northern Great Plains, the mountain communities of the Appalachians and the Ozarks, the worked-out mining towns scattered throughout the country, and on many of the reservations where a majority of the original inhabitants of this country live. The list of disadvantaged groups could be extended. The largest single such group is comprised of the more than 19,000,000 descendants of those Negroes who were brought here by force, robbed of their cultural heritage, reduced from the status of human beings to that of chattels, and only recently, as historic time goes, partially restored to human status and allowed to begin developing their personalities in line with our democratic heritage of belief in the right of every human being to "life, liberty and the pursuit of happiness."

There are others who may suffer handicaps from being included in the "minority" groups of the United States: those of Asian descent, Mexican-Americans, Indians, those from Puerto Rico and often their children, and, according to a recent study on discrimination in housing, those of the Jewish faith. These groups, the study showed, total "probably not fewer than 27,000,000 Americans, or nearly one-sixth of the national population, whose opportunities to live in neighborhoods of their choice are in some degree restricted because of their race, color or ethnic attachment."

Yes, our ancestors were builders—and we have continued in their tradition. We have also begun to correct some of their mistakes; we have begun to pay more attention to human values. In principle, we believe that every person, no matter what his background, should have a fair break. But we still have some distance to go in many fields in putting this principle into practice.

One reason the minorities are held back is the manner in which we of the "majority" view them and particularly in the ways we act or do not act where they are concerned. One of the worst ways to damage a member of a minority group is to label him or her with the presumed characteristics of the group as a whole. It is also one of the most widespread.

Perhaps a look at many of our ancestors in their early days will help us achieve a better perspective on how we can improve our democracy.

Chapter 2
OUR ANCESTORS AS STRANGERS

OUR Judaeo-Christian tradition counsels us to love the stranger "as thyself." Generally this does not happen. It is more likely to happen if the stranger belongs to our own racial, ethnic or nationality group, to our church, to our lodge, to our union, or at least to our own socio-economic class. This is because he is somewhat more likely to have been raised as we were raised, to "talk the same language," to have the same tastes, to have developed the same habits, the same reactions to daily events. In the vast majority of our daily actions we are creatures of habit; life would become a mass of intolerable choices in small matters if we were not. Trouble begins, in a society of rapid social change, when habits rule decisions on matters vitally affecting democracy and public issues. That is, trouble begins if we have not deliberately cultivated habits which are consonant with the democratic way of life in human relations.

Left to their own devices, our habits will often be guided by an insidious and universal fallacy known to scholars for years as *ethnocentrism*. This is an old synonym for "group centeredness." It has now been described and analyzed by social scientists and is understood to be part of the "natural" behavior of mankind. It is by applying intelligence and self and social control to "natural" actions that man becomes human, however. We now know that we must become aware of the process by which we acquire our habits, our feelings, our ideals, our ideas, and especially our assessment of "strangers." We must become aware of the fact that if a stranger comes from another ethnic, racial, nationality, religious, or class group he may well have habits, feelings, ideas, and ideals which do not coincide exactly with our own.

Often this is a painful process. It has proved to be such in our history. Unless two strangers can find or work out a common set of habits, feelings, ideas, and ideals to which they both owe allegiance, a neighborly life will be difficult. It is one of the encouraging signs of a maturing democracy that in the United States we are working out ways of achieving just such a solution to our human relations problems.

A look at what we have had to overcome may give us heart for the future, some ideas on how to proceed, and some warnings on what to guard against.

Names Do Hurt

The most common expression of ethnocentrism is *labeling:* it is found universally. "Sticks and stones may break my bones, but names will never hurt me." Children used to recite this little rhyme in self-defense, but names *do* hurt. They are particularly harmful when they injure the self-esteem of members of a minority group who are already struggling under great disadvantages to make their way in the world. Our forefathers had a deep and varied experience with name-calling. The "drunken" Irish, the "stuffed-shirt" Englishman, the "lazy" Negro, the "over-emotional" Italian, the "philandering" Frenchman, the "pushy" Jew, the "stingy" Scot: they have all appeared in our fiction and been heard on our stage and in our everyday life. Similarly, abroad, Americans are *"nouveaux riches,"* "over-ambitious," "uncultured," and "immature."

Thus, to the universal habit of labeling people we add the use of invidious adjectives. All members of a group of strangers—of persons not brought up the way we were—are conveniently classified and perhaps dismissed from our conscious thoughts. Our thinking-machine then delivers the adjective along with the noun the next time we hear "Italians," "Irish," or some other out-group mentioned.

For example, in 1859, some of our ancestors read newspaper articles which reported that "23 per cent of all the persons arrested in New York City were native Americans, 55 per cent were born in Ireland, 10 per cent in Germany, 7 per cent in England and Scotland and 5 per cent in other countries." Furthermore, seven-eighths of the persons committed to the city prison in 1850-58 were recorded as "intemperate." The picture of the drunken foreigner is thus easily understood. However, there are other facts which should be known.

First, even today not all persons arrested are convicted; often not even half are. There was a great deal of victimization of strangers by policemen who, as Robert Ernst points out, ". . . unwilling to risk their jobs by raiding gambling dens, brothels, and criminal hideouts, kept a sharp eye for slight misdemeanors committed by persons of no political influence." Many times the arrests were merely "on suspicion." Since a stranger in an area was almost always more highly visible than one of the neighbors, any unusual happening made him suspect.

Facts and Fallacies

Convictions are perhaps a more accurate reflection of crime in nationality groups. "Slightly less than one per cent of the native American population of New York City were convicted in 1859, while 5.5 per cent of the Irish, 3 per cent of the Scotch, 2.5 per cent of the English, 2 per cent of the Canadians, 1.5 per cent of the French and 1.2 per cent of the Germans were convicted." But there are other factors which must be considered. First, crimes overwhelmingly are committed by young people; in 1859, immigrants made up a large proportion of the age categories 20 to 40. Second, most of the crimes (aside from those arising out of drunkenness) involved theft and clearly arose in most cases out of need. There was, thus, a class factor which had to be considered. In other words, although the impression was widespread that it was *foreigners* who were committing the most crimes, a scientific analysis indicates that both age and class factors were more important than place of birth.

However, an even more serious fallacy was usually committed in discussing immigrants and crime. This was the fallacy of *judging* the group by unsound and unfair statistical comparisons. The answer to this fallacy is found in the comparative proportions of the convictions to the total population of each ethnic group. It is seen that even the most unfavorable conviction rate (5.5 per cent of the total Irish in New York City) means that almost 95 out of every 100 Irishmen in that year were *not* convicted of any crime—not even the drunkenness, rowdiness, fighting, boisterousness, etc., that "everybody knows" the Irish were "addicted to."

Whatever evidence of social and personal disorganization one chooses, the newcomer at the bottom of the income ladder showed it in plenty. Deaths from all causes between 1840 and 1858 (especially tuberculosis, typhus, typhoid, cholera, pneumonia, bronchitis, and scrofula) were overwhelmingly greater among the recent immigrants who lived in the three-fourths of New York City which were slums. Much was made of the fact that the Irish made up 54 per cent of the city's foreign-born population in 1855 but accounted for 85 per cent of the foreign-born admitted to Bellevue, the city hospital, between 1849 and 1859. The Germans (both Jewish and non-Jewish), on the other hand, had a much better record, with a proportion of 29.4 per cent of the population and 6.2 per cent of the hospital admissions. It must be noted, however, that they were in much more comfortable circumstances when they came to New York and lived in much better housing, comparatively, than did the Irish. Another important factor was a higher level of education among the Germans, which saved them from exploitation by medical quacks.

Nevertheless, there were Germans whose disease, death, and pauperism rates matched those of the Irish. They were those from rural areas whose occupation was searching rubbish heaps for rags, paper, food, or anything else salvageable. From this unpalatable occupation they too, in time, moved up the economic ladder leaving the latest immigrant group, the Italians, to take their place. By 1890, the German had become, as one writer put it, "the thrifty tradesman or the prosperous farmer of today."

It is instructive to note that the distribution of perpetrators of assaults tried in the New York courts in 1907 and 1908, just 50 years after the statistics previously examined, showed that the Irish, the Germans, and the English, so prominent a half-century before, had dropped down the scale considerably, and had been replaced by the Italians as the chief ethnic group displaying signs of personal and social disorganization.

The 1908 *United States Census Report on Prisoners* directly approached the question of the supposed greater criminality of the foreign-born. It said that ". . . immigration has not increased the volume of crime to a distinguishable extent, if at all"; indeed, it reported that the percentage of immigrants among prisoners had actually fallen between 1890 and 1904, and that native Americans "exhibited in general a tendency to commit more serious crimes than did the immigrant."

Many of the statements made about various ethnic groups involved a belief in some innate characteristic with which the members of a particular group were born. Even the tenement house reformer, Jacob Riis, wrote that the Italians and the Russian and Polish Jews, ". . . differing hopelessly in much, have this in common: they carry their slums with them wherever they go, if allowed to do it . . . [they] rise only by compulsion."

Just a few pages later, ironically, the famous crusader against slums pointed out that where a landlord fought every improvement of conditions for his Italian tenants, he characterized them as a "bad lot," whereas across the street another landlord reported that the Italians were "good tenants." Much of the comment on our ancestors would seem to follow this example, one of the most widespread of logical fallacies: reasoning from insufficient data.

Something was found wrong with each group that came. The English immigrants, for instance, were considered "the worst type of worker" by many factory managers, despite the fact that their skill levels were higher than those of workers of other nationalities. The trouble was that this made them more "independent," more willing to shift to more promising jobs, and more interested in union organization!

Much of the misunderstanding of the stranger was due to the differences between his customs and habits and those of older Americans. Reactions toward his behavior ranged from mild amusement at some differences to denunciations such as "disgusting"—particularly when bodily or household cleanliness was involved. Generally, however, the stranger was accepted as a person who had come to better himself, just as the previous newcomer had done.

Xenophobia

There is another tendency which has ebbed and flowed—sometimes focusing on one ethnic or racial group, and sometimes on another.

The Greeks had a word for it—*xenophobia.* It is a malady known to psychiatry as "a morbid dread of meeting strangers," but this definition does not convey all the danger which the term implies. Xenophobia affects communities as well as individuals. It exists in mild or extreme form in most parts of the world, sometimes in epidemic proportions. It becomes more menacing as rapid transportation brings the peoples of the world closer together physically. Although it is by no means necessarily the only, or even the most basic, cause of undemocratic or otherwise bad human relations, the disease is surely one cause that must be diagnosed and treated if good human relations are to be established.

Xenophobia is insidious—a person may suffer from it without knowing he is ill. The symptoms are well-known, however, and awareness of its treacherous character is the beginning of the cure. The person affected by fear of strangers may act somewhat like a victim of malaria: he may have chills and fever in the presence of an unfamiliar person or group.

From time to time such epidemics have marked American life. The middle of the past century saw anti-Irish, anti-Catholic riots in many of the industrial cities of the Northeast. The "Know Nothing" party, basically an anti-immigrant group, was organized and within a short time elected seven governors, 43 congressmen, and five senators.

Abraham Lincoln was moved to exclaim:

> Our progress in degeneracy appears to me to be pretty rapid. As a nation we began by declaring that "All men are created equal." We now practically read it, "All men are created equal, except Negroes." When the Know-Nothings get control, it will read, "All men are created equal, except Negroes and foreigners and Catholics." When it comes to this, I shall prefer emigrating to some country where they make no pretense of liberty—to Russia, for instance, where despotism can be taken pure, and without the base alloy of hypocrisy.

Since that time, the Ku Klux Klan and many similar movements for "100 per cent Americanism" have shown their fears by damning Negroes, Catholics, and Jews, specifically, and "foreigners," generally. Ironically, the disease often attacks those whose ancestors were themselves under attack as foreigners.

Nativists vs. "New" Immigrants

Late in the past century, many Americans began to look upon the strangers of the past with fond memories while the "new" stranger was looked upon with suspicion. One of the greatest contributors to this shift was Francis A. Walker, president of the Massachusetts Institute of Technology, who misapplied Darwinian concepts to the social struggle and came out with the following formulation which carried great influence. The "new" immigrants, he contended, ". . . are beaten men from beaten races; representing the worst failures in the struggle for existence. They have none of the ideas and aptitudes which . . . belong to those who are descended from the tribes that met under the oak trees of old Germany to make laws and choose chieftains."

Soon there was an outpouring of articles and speeches "proving" that the particular branch of the white race which had settled in Northwestern Europe (the so-called Nordics) had a virtual monopoly on the wit and wisdom, the political, social, and economic abilities of the world.

The more humanitarian of the increasingly vociferous "nativists," while demanding that further immigration be restricted to those as fortunate as themselves in their choice of ancestors, also felt that it was part of the "white man's burden" to carry the advantages of Anglo-Saxon civilization to the "lesser breeds without the Law." They exerted an extremely harmful influence by offsetting the democratic forces in the country which were opposed to the imperialist ventures that gave us such colonial possessions as Puerto Rico, the Philippine Islands, Hawaii, Guam, and the Panama Canal.

The new eugenics movement backed up the racist pseudo-science which proved that "new" immigrants were "unassimilable." The "Yellow Peril" of the early 1900's; the patriotic fears and hysteria of World War I; the post-war reaction; all contributed to strengthening xenophobic tendencies. One result was the high-pressure "Americanization" campaign with its widespread damage to the self-esteem of the not-yet-naturalized immigrant. Another was the Immigration Restriction Act of 1924. It was a direct expression of the marriage of racist and nationalistic feelings. It has since been amended to strike out the Oriental exclusion policy which played so well into Japan's hands in that country's anti-United States drive in Asia. Essentially, however, as the then-Senator John F. Kennedy pointed out in his pamphlet written for the Anti-Defamation League, *A Nation of Immigrants,* it is still racist in intent.

This restrictive act, along with the depression which followed within a few years, cut immigration down to a comparative trickle. The in-bound total for the decade 1901-10 had been 8,795,386; the following ten years had shown a drop to 5,735,811, partly because of war difficulties. The 1921-30 period showed a further drop to

4,107,209, but in the 1931-40 decade, in-migration fell to 528,431, which was more than counterbalanced by out-migration. Italians, Poles, Yugoslavs, and many others fled the rigors of the depression for their original homes.

There was a sequel to immigration restriction which was not at all foreseen. That is our next concern.

Chapter 3
THE CONTEMPORARY STRANGER

Ambition, hope, courage, and differential economic opportunities are the four major ingredients in the voluntary movement of peoples from their native soil to new and strange areas. The 43,000,000 immigrants of the past have written this lesson large on the pages of our history. Their coming sometimes overshadows in our minds and in public discussion the fact that we were a century ago—and still are today—a people on the move.

We are more mobile than our ancestors were a century ago, during the great Westward movement. As the following table shows, each year an average of almost one out of every five persons in the United States has moved his home.

Internal Migration in the United States *

Persons Moving Their Home

Year	Total No. of Persons	Within Same State	From One State To Another
1952-53	30,786,000	25,264,000	5,522,000
1953-54	29,027,000	23,993,000	5,034,000
1954-55	31,492,000	26,597,000	4,895,000
1955-56	33,098,000	28,045,000	5,053,000
1956-57	31,834,000	26,758,000	5,076,000
1957-58	33,263,000	27,679,000	5,584,000
1958-59	32,804,000	27,734,000	5,070,000
1959-60	33,811,000	28,288,000	5,523,000
1960-61	35,535,000	29,782,000	5,753,000
1961-62	34,364,000	28,802,000	5,562,000

* *Statistical Abstract of the United States*

Each recent year, some 30,000,000 persons have moved; about 5,000,000 across county lines and about 5,000,000 more across state lines. Two out of five of the latter usually move across regional lines. Furthermore, the process had been speeding up even before World War II. The total moving from one county to another in the decade 1921-30, for example, was only 9,000,000; during the five-year period 1936-40, it had risen to 14,000,000.

More than one-half of the 3,072 counties in the United States lost population between 1950 and 1960. Twenty-eight states had a net out-migration in the same period.

Neither losses nor gains were capricious; all can be understood by examining economic conditions and demographic realities. Areas of low economic opportunity are invariably areas of high fertility. Migration flows from such areas to those of better economic development.

The nation as a whole gains by this movement, in spite of economic, social, and family dislocations involved in widespread migration. Workers who could not hope to advance much faster or further than they have at home are attracted by greater possibilities in areas of more rapid development. The major areas of out-migration lie in the Midwest and the Deep South; the major areas of in-migration are in the Western, Eastern and North Central States. These are the areas showing the highest per capita income, the greatest development of manufacturing and other sources of wealth, the lowest rates of illiteracy, the lowest birth and death rates, and other indices of economic and social advancement.

One of the reasons for the encouraging rise in average income in recent years is the large-scale internal migration. The figures on median family income show average income at $1,325 in 1939; $3,107 in 1949; $5,050 in 1958; and $7,054 in 1962.

A study of migrants from West Virginia showed those moving out of the state between 1953 and 1955 increased their annual income by $1,024. All other migrant streams show similar results.

Such mobility is now widely recognized as beneficial to the worker, to employers, and to the entire national economy. A *Life* editorial headline puts it succinctly: "Full Employment Means Full Mobility." It continues, "Labor Department figures show that workers who move get notably higher incomes than workers who stay put." The scholarly Committee for Economic Development in its work on *Economic Growth in the United States* stresses "a high degree of mobility" as a notable characteristic of our labor force, concluding that the "immense historical shift of labor from less productive to more productive uses itself tended to push up output per man-hour in the economy as a whole."

The major regions of the country themselves show a pattern of internal population redistribution which is extremely important in our economic, social, and political life. Everywhere rural areas have lost population to the cities. The farm population dropped by 16,234,000 persons in the years 1940-62; from 23.2 per cent to 7.7 per cent of the total population. But there was a migration from farms of 23,879,000 persons during the same period. The difference is accounted for by the high natural increase characteristic of most rural areas.

There are now 213 Standard Metropolitan Statistical Areas in the conterminous United States and their population is growing at a much higher rate, 18.5 per cent, than that of the 48 states as a whole. It rose from 89,316,903 in 1950 to 112,885,175 in 1960, or by 26 per cent, on the basis of their 1950 boundaries. Several of them grew substantially through annexation of surrounding areas.

Again, just as there are different patterns of growth inside regions, there are quite different patterns within the metropolitan area. The central city for years has been growing at a slower rate than the suburbs, as the following table shows:

Differential Growth Inside U.S. Metropolitan Areas: 1920-1960

Period	Central City	Outside Central City
1921-30	23.0%	43.6%
1931-40	4.7	14.4
1941-50	12.1	37.1
1951-60	1.5	61.7

(Annexations occurring between 1950 and 1960 are ignored in this table to emphasize the essential trend. If they were accounted for, the increase in central cities would be 8.2 per cent and outside them, 47.2 per cent.)

There *is* one big difference in motivation between the rural-urban or South-North migrations on the one hand, and the central city-suburban migration on the other. Migrants in the former stream are motivated largely by a *search* for greater economic success; movers to suburbia make the shift largely as a *result* of economic success. The former move into the city to start climbing the occupational ladder. The latter step out of the city from the higher rungs of the ladder. (Often their own experience of rejection by their new neighbors in the suburbs is just as bitter as is that of the poor migrant entering the central city.)

This process must be seen in the context of urban decay, which follows more or less the same lines throughout all Western countries. Neighborhoods near the central core of the city are allowed to deteriorate as it becomes less and less profitable to keep buildings repaired for the inhabitants who originally occupied them. It becomes increasingly profitable to turn them into boardinghouses. Universally, it is recognized that the appearance of a boardinghouse marks the beginning of the end of an era, and of the neighborhood as a desirable residential area, unless the community can be organized to maintain minimum standards.

"Get-rich-quick" promoters play on both the fears and the cupidity of the owners. A widely known technique, called "block-busting" by the real estate trade, is often used to panic home-owners into selling at a loss. Rentals in deteriorating neighborhoods are often fantastically profitable. Square-foot rentals are generally greater by far than for better housing. For instance, in New York City, elevator apartments on Central Park West which are in excellent condition rent for about one-half as much per square foot as run-down housing a few buildings away in the transition zone.

When new people move into a neighborhood in fairly large numbers, its social composition is likely to change in the following characteristics: age, family size and structure, education, major occupations, religious affiliation, political beliefs, and ethnic makeup. Obviously, repercussions will spread into every aspect of life.

The movement of "non-whites" gets most of the headlines, just as the arrival of the newest, and most highly visible, stranger got attention in the past. However, of all the 44,691,064 persons found by the 1960 census to be living in a state other than their state of birth, only 11.1 per cent were non-white: 5,445,965 compared with 39,245,099 whites. The 5,753,000 interstate migrants in the 1960-61 Current Population Survey period (*supra,* p. 28) contained 464,000 non-whites; slightly over 8 per cent.

Negro Migration

It is Negro migration, however, which probably causes more hysterical reactions than all other internal migration. Emotions run even higher than they did against the "refuse from foreign countries" in the past. When the Negro migrates, he finds barriers at every turn. He is shunted into the most disreputable areas of the city just as our ancestors were. Often he is denied access to the facilities which could help him solve his problems. The physical and social situation in which he finds himself results in higher general death rates than in the white population, higher tuberculosis rates, and an expectancy of life which lags seven to eight years behind that of whites.

Materially, the Negro has made progress, as is indicated, among other facts, by the narrowing of the gap between white and Negro death rates. The expectancy of life at birth for white babies in 1900 was 14.6 years longer than that of Negro babies; in 1960 the gap had been reduced to seven years.

The Negro is moving from the farms to the cities; only 27 per cent remained on farms in 1960. He is moving from the South to the North and West, though 60 per cent were still in the South in 1960. Both moves give him greater occupational advantages for himself and greater educational advantages for his children. Negroes are still suffering in their new locations from confinement to the lowest rungs of the occupational ladder, the less desirable jobs, the part-time and seasonal work; the jobs most vulnerable to fluctuations in the economic system; the positions which carry less pay and therefore less prestige.

They suffer also from the fact that so often they are paid less for doing the same work. Even though there was a substantially greater proportionate increase in the income of non-white male workers than of whites in the past 20 years, the former stood at 60 per cent of the latter in 1960. It had fallen to 55 per cent by 1962. The income of Southern non-whites stood at 40 per cent of the whites in 1960. And the differential between the races among female workers was even greater.

Both white and non-white groups have suffered mental and emotional damage from the attitudes and actions of the dominant whites. This was recognized in the 1954 Supreme Court decision outlawing school segregation, and in the historic Civil Rights Law of 1964.

However, discrimination, often involving the violence of lynching or the mass murder and wholesale destruction by mobs, has had a long history in this country. Race riots in East St. Louis and

Detroit and several in Chicago indicate that it is not simply the heritage of slavery which is responsible. Competition for jobs, for housing, for space in schools—all have played a role. Extremely important also was xenophobia, inflamed by the legacy of the racists who had "proved" that the Negro was inherently inferior under the laws of God. They thereby eased the consciences of the slave owners who were trying to think of themselves as Christians.

The heritage of slavery aside, in his search for a more satisfactory life, the Negro today faces many of the same kinds of attacks faced by our ancestors.

From Farm to City

Not all of the non-whites are Negroes. The Indians, original occupants of the territory conquered by the white man, now make up a sizable minority in the internal migrant stream. There are scatterings of Asians also. Some areas think primarily of these two groups when the stranger is mentioned. Other areas think of the Mexican-American, who is included in the white category, and still others think of French-Canadians. It does not matter which group is being described; the language has not changed significantly since most of our almost 43,000,000 ancestors arrived decades ago.

Try an experiment! The following are excerpts from reports on migrants to a big city. What group do you think is being discussed?

> They are satisfied with poor living conditions. . . . They don't want modern facilities. . . . They won't use bathtubs. . . . They don't want to change their standards. . . . They're destructive and overspend money. . . . We've known about any number of illegitimate children who have moved into already overcrowded homes with the mother. I recall a family with thirteen children of its own. Sister has four illegitimate children. . . .
>
> "Have little regard for education for themselves or for children. . . . Adults often regard school authorities as a threat. . . . It is difficult to get these people to do any learning. . . . I have found children with a three-year vocabulary, although they were about six years old. . . . Our only problems of truancy have been with this group. . . . Education does not have importance to these people as it does to us. . . ." and so forth.

Reports from another city about the same group include such phrases as:

> Often removing screens, they sit half-dressed where it is cooler, and dispose of garbage the quickest way. . . . When it comes to sex, their habits—with respect to such matters as incest and statutory rape—are clearly at variance with urban legal requirements.

Both discussions are of the purest "Nordics" in the United States: the white, Protestant, individualistic Southern mountaineer, in Cincinnati and Chicago, respectively. They are descendants of those whom Thomas Jefferson looked upon as the backbone of democracy: "the chosen people of God, if ever He had a chosen people."

The difficulties reported obviously have nothing to do with color, creed, language, or nationality. They are complicated by "labeling," however. Much to the distress of thousands of Southern-born white persons who have migrated to Chicago and Cincinnati, they find themselves being judged by the deeds of the minority of their group which finds itself in trouble with the police, the schools, or the social agencies.

There are at least two-and-one-half million persons of Mexican descent living in the United States, mostly in Texas, Arizona, New Mexico, and California. There has been considerable migration from farm to city within these states as well as movement into other areas. Their difficulties are the familiar ones of handicaps on their part (lack of English, lack of skills, poor health arising out of their disadvantaged status for decades, etc.) complicated by stereotyping, prejudice, and discrimination. Many restaurants will not serve "greasers," even though they may be well-dressed; beauty parlors may refuse to prettify even the chic secretary in a Mexican consulate; the D. A. R. in one town objected to letting the honor student in a local high school carry the United States flag in the Memorial Day parade because of his Mexican parentage; and denial of burial rights to a United States veteran of Mexican ancestry became a *cause célèbre* a few years ago which was happily resolved when the President of the United States ordered him buried with military honors in Arlington. Discrimination in housing, schooling, employment, civil rights, and many other fields has been somewhat diminished by court action and by civic, labor union, and political participation in recent years.

That there is a long way to go is indicated by such an index as the comparative tuberculosis death rates per 100,000 population in San Antonio, Texas, in 1948-50: Anglo-Americans, 37;

Negroes, 70; Mexican-Americans, 125! Tuberculosis death rates are a most sensitive indication of living conditions, especially of overcrowding in housing and other aspects of the combination of low income and discrimination.

The highest tuberculosis rates in the United States are found in many of the communities occupied by those who were here long before the rest of us came as strangers—the American Indian. Some of the greatest difficulties in adjustment to urban environments are also found among those Indians who leave their home communities, often at the urging of the United States government. Minneapolis, with about 7,000 Indians, made a study of some of their adjustment difficulties. A meaningful summary of the situation is found in the local health department comparison of average age at death:

All Minneapolis residents	68 years
All Indians in Minnesota	46 years
Indians living in Minneapolis	37 years

A report on their housing conditions is reminiscent of Jacob Riis and other reporters on our ancestors:

> One Indian family of five or six, living in two rooms, will take in relatives and friends who come from the reservation seeking jobs until perhaps fifteen people will be crowded into the space. In one case sixteen people, of all ages including infants, were found in one unventilated attic room with no furnishings but the electric plate, and blankets and clothing.

Welfare cases, arrests for drunkenness, difficulties in school, etc., also sound familiar. Again, however, we ask, "How many Indians are we talking about when we lump all Indians together and generalize about their conduct *on the basis of those arrested?*" A Minneapolis police judge gave an answer which, although not statistically established, is the estimate of a perceptive person acquainted with the circumstances:

> Due to failure over the years to get any response, and due to their mistrust of us, it has been very difficult to work with the Indians through our probation office, although we have tried many times. As a consequence most of these offenders end up in the workhouse. It is the feeling of the court that over a long period of time the

percentage of Indians appearing in the police court will run from 14 per cent to 20 per cent.

Again, even though it is a large proportion of all Indians in Minneapolis, it is still only one out of seven, or one out of five at the most.

The newest strangers in many parts of the United States are our fellow citizens from Puerto Rico. They have been coming for many years. Even before the United States took the island from Spain in 1898 for the purpose of providing a bastion to protect the Panama Canal then being planned, there were Puerto Ricans in New York City. Sixty years before that, in 1838, the Cuban and Puerto Rican merchants in New York City financed the Spanish Benevolent Society to help strangers arriving from Spain and her colonies and former colonies in the New World. They and their descendants helped finance revolutionary activities in Cuba and Puerto Rico to overthrow Spanish domination. It is not of these early Puerto Rican citizens or their descendants that we usually speak, however, when we refer to the Puerto Ricans living in the United States.

Chapter 4
THE PUERTO RICAN AS A STRANGER

THE experiences of our Puerto Rican fellow citizen, newly arrived from his home in the Caribbean, parallel quite closely the experiences of our own ancestors and of other contemporary strangers. Compared with either previous or present immigration or with the other contemporary internal migration, his numbers are small. But they have been greatly exaggerated by sensationalists and xenophobes.

One daily newspaper's headline in 1946 was "Tidal Wave of Puerto Ricans Swamping City." The net migration to the mainland United States in 1945 was 13,573; in 1946 it was 39,911. The figure of 710,000 Puerto Ricans in New York City was used by another paper in 1948 (when the total was about 180,000) and a few years later, still another paper reported, "there are an estimated 2,000,000 Puerto Ricans living in the nation's largest city." That year, 1953, there were around 448,000, if 100,000 children born in New York City of Puerto Rican parentage were included. The reason for these inaccuracies is well understood by social psychologists and psychiatrists; they call it "perceptual accentuation." A valuable study of attitudes of rehabilitation caseworkers found another illuminating illustration of this process. Workers in one agency estimated their Puerto Rican caseload at 75 per cent of all clients. They were greatly surprised when they were told the correct proportion was 30 per cent. Frequently, estimates even by professionally trained personnel ran two to three times the real figure.

The writer found the same phenomenon in Great Britain, where in one industrial city the number of migrants from the West Indies was variously estimated by responsible persons at from 5,000 to 40,000. The higher "visibility" of the stranger may arise from speech, clothing, color, behavior, or other factors. The significant point is that the stranger *is* generally more visible than other citizens.

It is important to know the facts about the ebb and flow of migration from Puerto Rico. The figures are those of the United States Immigration and Naturalization Service office in San Juan and represent the difference between all persons who leave Puerto Rico during each calendar year and those who return during the same year. Since it represents total outflow from Puerto Rico to all points, it may slightly exaggerate the number coming to the United States. The data are available since the fiscal year 1907-08 and are plotted in Figure I by the shaded area to show how the movement has fluctuated.

The size of the Puerto Rican migration varies closely with job opportunities in the United States as reflected in the close relationship between the migration and U.S. national income.

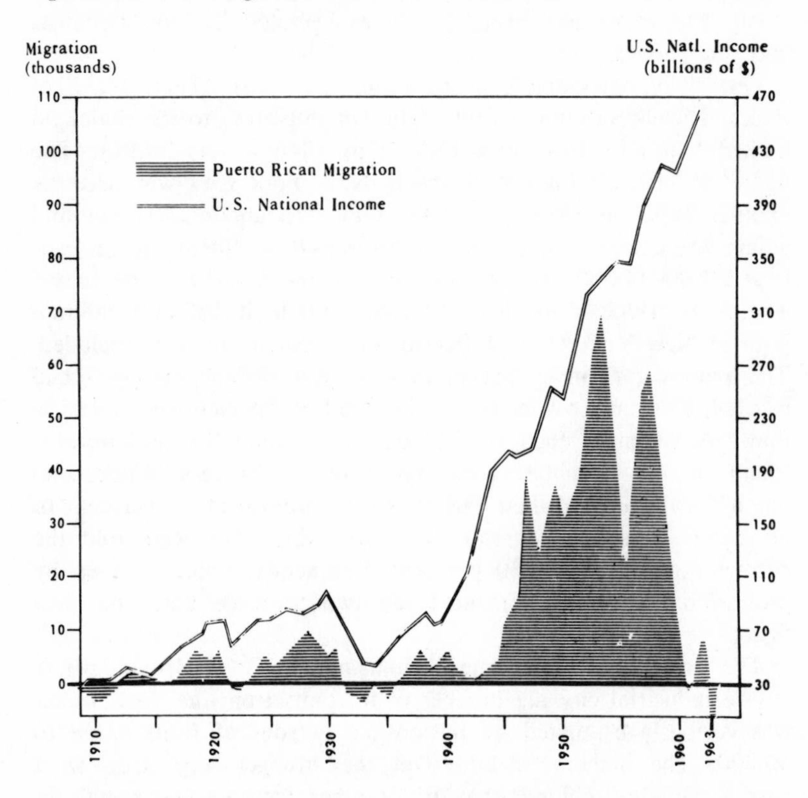

Puerto Rican Migration to the Continental United States

Annual Averages

1909-30	1,986	1941-50	18,794
1931-40	904	1951-60	41,212
		1961-63	3,567

Each Year, 1946-1963

1946	39,911	1955	45,464
1947	24,551	1956	52,315
1948	32,775	1957	37,704
1949	25,698	1958	27,690
1950	34,703	1959	29,989
1951	52,899	1960	16,298
1952	59,103	1961	−1,754 *
1953	69,124	1962	10,800
1954	21,531	1963	−5,479 *

* The minus figure represents a net outflow.

The solid line indicates the ups and downs of employment as reflected in the national income. It is obvious that migration is highly sensitive to business conditions. In other words, when more Puerto Ricans are needed for our economic system, they come; if fewer are needed, fewer come. There was, in fact, a net reverse flow during the depressions of 1907-09, 1920-21, and in the 1930's. The 1948-49 reduction in jobs resulted in a 22 per cent drop in migration from the island; economic conditions in late 1953 and 1954 caused an over-the-year drop in migration to the mainland of 68.8 per cent. Increased demand for labor began to reflect itself in an upturn in Puerto Rican migration during the third quarter of 1955, and the total for the year was 45,464. Migration during 1956 reflected continued improvement in job opportunities and reached 52,315 for the year. The downturn which began the next year caused a drop in the flow for 1957 of 28 per cent, to a total of 37,704. A further drop of 27 per cent was registered in 1958, with the figure for that year 27,690. Migration rose only slightly in 1959, with the improvement in job conditions, to 29,989. It dropped to 16,298 in 1960; and in 1961 there was again a net return to Puerto Rico of 1,754. The upward flow reached 10,800 in 1962, but 1963 again saw a net flow to the island of 5,479. It is believed the migration will now level off somewhere between the

1962 and 1963 figures, unless unemployment sharply increases here.

Two factors have in recent years reduced the sensitivity of U.S. national income as an indicator of Puerto Rican migration. First, automation is making it possible for us to maintain rising income in spite of high unemployment. Second, job opportunities in Puerto Rico itself are attracting migration from the States, both of Puerto Ricans and other citizens. There has also been a migration of about 16,000 Cubans to Puerto Rico via the United States since Castro's revolution. Many refugee entrepreneurs have rebuilt their businesses in Puerto Rico.

The Puerto Rican migration rose sharply at the end of World War II as a result of a combination of drastic labor shortages in the States and improved transportation between San Juan and New York City. Puerto Rico was largely isolated from the States during the war by the German submarines in nearby waters; airplane transportation was still in its infancy. Labor force demands in the States led to a demand for faster and cheaper air passage.

One result was that the airplane, in effect, drew the island occupied by the Commonwealth of Puerto Rico close to the United States. The Commonwealth's labor force has now become part of the labor force of the whole country.

Most newcomers from Puerto Rico are in almost exactly the position occupied by the majority of our ancestors. They are relegated to the worst (and most expensive) housing; they hold the lowest-paying jobs; their children attend overcrowded schools; they are exploited by unscrupulous landlords, "easy-credit" merchants, and racketeers; they suffer winter temperatures and even more chilling social contacts; they are deluged with the same verbal brickbats once showered on our ancestors; and, finally, teen-age groups, already in possession of their "turf," are ready to kill the newcomers, if necessary, to maintain their sovereignty.

There are, also, the professional xenophobes, those who hate almost everybody—probably including themselves. Typical of the published mouthings of this group are the following:

> . . . subject to congenital tropical diseases . . . we don't want others' peelings and leavings unless they are Puerto Ricans who can vote, or Sicilians who can be enlisted into the good works of their older compatriots . . . almost impossible to assimilate . . . few can obtain employment . . . they turn to guile and wile and the steel blade, the traditional weapon of the sugar cane cutter, mark of their blood and

> heritage . . . these animals . . . the lure was relief . . . In the last 20 years some 600,000 of the little Brown Brothers have been funneled into our town, mostly in East Harlem . . . not all Puerto Ricans are dusky like those in New York, despite the propaganda sold by professional racists of the Roosevelt stamp . . . the most vicious element in New York life . . .

Here are all the classical tricks of the demagogue—lies, exaggerations, slighting references to skin color, imputation of hereditary disabilities, lumping with others who were given a bad name, racist slogans accompanied by the labeling of a political opponent as "racist," and others.

The language of the demagogue is replaced by the language of the gutter in the anonymous letters received by the author after every radio or television discussion in which he participates or after a statement in a newspaper. Most of these letters contain phrases too filthy for quotation. Here is a favorite (with original spelling intact):

> So you are one of those ———— that are bringing those monkey faced animals into this country. I consider a Puerto Rican lower than a pig. Those dirty black faced diseased dogs they are a menace to descent people. I pray with all my might a violet death overtakes you. I am going to do everything in my power to fight them everybody I have spoken to hates there sight. Those knife carrying ————. They loused up every neighborhood in N. Y.

Another, typical of many, refers to the author as "full of Latin baloney from the Vatican. The trouble is that there is too much expected of these members of the monkey family who have been jerked out of the jungle with an ignorance that only the Roman Catholic teachings of uneducated priests know."

These "nut" letters might easily be shrugged off as the work of a few psychopaths. However, they display, although in extreme form, the kind of verbal reactions which are too widely heard. The urge to do violence against the stranger lies just below the surface in the individual who has such an emotional reaction.

The urge to violence isn't always controlled. *The New York Post* of March 25, 1957, carries an example under the heading: "'We Were Talking in Spanish'—and the Words Meant Death." A Puerto Rican veteran just discharged from the Army was drinking a beer with his brother to celebrate starting his first civilian job.

Other occupants of the Brooklyn bar objected to Spanish being used; result, the veteran went to his grave instead of a new job—his head kicked to pieces by a crowd after he had been floored by a blow from behind.

Stereotypes and "Loaded" Words

Less vicious in intent are those who fall into the habit of generalizing from the actions of the most highly visible of the newest group of strangers and build up stereotypes which they then apply to the entire group. These disparaging pictures of the newcomer often interfere with his making a reasonably prompt adjustment to his new situation. Sometimes the stereotype blocks the kind of action which may be necessary to protect the health or even the lives of members of the minority. *The New York Times* reported on April 22, 1958, for example, that Puerto Rican sewing machine operators in a Manhattan loft factory began to act hysterically one morning. Some screamed, some fainted, some cried, some started running for the fire escape. A physician who was summoned advised that "Puerto Ricans are a very high-tensioned people," so nothing needed to be done. Someone else called the fire and health departments which discovered that "a very high, deadly concentration of carbon monoxide" was seeping into the workshop. Continued exposure might well have meant many deaths.

There are more subtle ways of expressing rejection. The use of "loaded" words when writing of those already struggling against great odds to find their place in the world is particularly unfortunate. Recently a report on migration was published in which the authors referred to "thousands upon thousands of Southern Negroes *swarming* to the Northern industrial cities." Puerto Rico, it said, "has become the most prolific *spawning* ground for the American migrant." (Italics supplied.) It is interesting to note the use of terms usually applied only to animals.

The term "the Puerto Rican problem" is another example of the heedless use of words which hurt, which give another blow to the self-esteem of those who move from Puerto Rico to the States.

The "visible" Puerto Rican, especially when he is on or near the bottom of the economic ladder, has problems, just as other poor people have problems. There are no characteristic problems which the Puerto Rican has to carry alone; all that he has he shares with thousands of others in other ethnic groups, and they all share them with our ancestors.

Comparisons of today's conditions with a supposedly better past also add to the psychic burden the new stranger must carry. The immigrants of the past, it is true, brought different customs, lived in poverty, spoke another language, etc. But, the argument runs, "they formed little Italies, Irelands, Germanies, Polands, Hungaries and Jewries"—i.e., ghettos—and "out of sight was out of mind." This description might be true if New York City at any one moment in the past were photographed and that static picture were taken as the reality. Actually, New York or any other city or social structure is always in the process of change, of growth and of decay.

Yesterday and Today

Let us take 1890, when Jacob Riis reported that "the tenements today *are* New York, harboring three-quarters of its population." He asked, "Where are the tenements of today? Say rather: where are they not? In fifty years they have crept up from the Fourth Ward slums and the Five Points the whole length of the island, and have polluted the Annexed District [the Bronx] to the Westchester line. Crowding all the lower wards, wherever business leaves a foot of ground unclaimed; strung along both rivers, like ball and chain tied to the foot of every street, and filling up Harlem with their restless, pent-up multitudes, they hold within their clutch the wealth and business of New York, hold them at their mercy in the day of mob-rule and wrath."

Against this background, one wonders at the statement made to a large social work gathering in 1957 by a famous anthropologist that the immigrants of the past, in contrast to the Puerto Ricans today, "did not invade the school rooms en masse, they did not move into neighborhoods occupied by the older residents and render them undesirable, they did not fill all the public conveyances."

The reference to the transportation system is ironic in view of a 1928 essay by the prominent writer Albert Jay Nock which contains the following references to a "dreadful people" in New York: "I sometimes think there will be a record-breaking pogrom in New York some day, and there are occasions even now when the most peace-loving person among us wishes he could send over a couple of *sotnias* of Cossacks to floor-manage the subway rush."

The use of the word "invade" by the anthropologist cited above is interesting in this connection. A whole school of sociologists has built a "social ecology" with neighborhood "invasion" by a strange group as one of its major concepts. This group is located at the University of Chicago, and its major research has been done in that city. The first work of these sociologists dates from the 1920's. Thus, New York's present difficulties in neighborhood transitions are neither new nor confined to New York. Similar studies have been made in many cities with roughly similar results, no matter what the ethnic group involved.

Who Is to Blame?

There is also a type of verbal brickbat arising out of misplaced responsibility. This approach blames the victim for the situation in which he finds himself. An outstanding clubwoman several years ago made the statement that "the slum problem was almost solved before we allowed the Puerto Ricans to roll into the city like a plague of locusts." This statement not only indicates a lack of knowledge of the situation, but contains harmful "loaded" words and a scapegoat theory of housing which cannot be supported by facts. Neither New York City nor any other large city in the United States has ever come anywhere near "almost solving" its slum problem. When the statement appeared, reliable estimates were that New York City was a little better off than the nation as a whole, in which approximately 24 per cent of all dwelling units were substandard. New York City's slum dwellers were estimated at 20 per cent of its population. The Puerto Ricans at that time made up 5 per cent of the total population. In other words, there were three times as many non-Puerto Ricans as Puerto Ricans living in slums, even on the false assumption that *all* Puerto Ricans lived in slums. But there are indications that even this proportion is too high. In the same year the Mayor's Committee on Housing reported that "one-third of the city's slums are occupied by minority families who constitute some 12 per cent of the population." Since Puerto Ricans made up less than half the city's minorities, they would, therefore, be occupying less than one-sixth of the slums.

Exploitation by "slumlords" goes on today. The words of Jacob

Riis are still valid: "Estate owners and agents of property perceived that a greater percentage of profits could be realized by the conversion of houses and blocks into barracks and dividing their space into smaller proportions. . . . Blocks were rented of owners, or 'purchased on time,' or taken in charge at a percentage, and held for under-letting." From that time to this, slum properties have been "gold mines" for the person who knows how to "work" them. The slum tenants on the west side of New York City, for instance, pay an average of $2.10 per square foot for their hovels while the inhabitants of the well-maintained elevator apartments within a block or two on Central Park West average $1.02. The number of persons crowded into the old brownstones gives the owner a return of 12 to 14 per cent on his purchase price; it also provides profits for a superstructure of bankers, mortgage companies, and private speculative lenders.

An idea of the horror in store for slum inhabitants is furnished by stories from Chicago and New York City on children bitten by rats. New York's Health Commissioner announced a few years ago that "New York has as many rats as it has people" and that 565 persons had been reported bitten during 1958, most of them in Manhattan. In 1957 the total for that borough alone was approximately 500. Of these about 300 had Spanish names. There were bites reported from 350 blocks; only non-Spanish names appeared in 167 blocks, only Spanish in 153 blocks, and both in 30 blocks. Spanish-speaking citizens are obviously not the only ones struck by the afflictions of the slums.

Color Discrimination

In his new environment, the Puerto Rican suffers from the effects of a virulent form of a disease which in Puerto Rico exists only spottily and then mostly in a mild form—color discrimination. One recent scientific study of Puerto Rico reports that "on the main avenues of life there is little attention paid to skin color." A dark skin may handicap one somewhat, but there is at least as much vestigial class feeling as color prejudice in what little discrimination takes place. There are no such major differences in life chances associated with skin color in Puerto Rico as are reflected in differential birth, death, and morbidity rates in the States.

The Puerto Rican stranger therefore gets enmeshed in a situation he usually doesn't understand. He is told by law enforcement officers in some cities that he must "stay away from the Negroes." But this doesn't make sense to him; at home one stayed away from bad people and made friends with those who acted decently. "Are all the Negroes bad people?" a Puerto Rican in one city asked a policeman who had just given the above-mentioned warning. Startled, the policeman had to think a moment before he answered, "No, of course not, they are just like anybody else—some are bad and some are good." "All right," replied the Puerto Rican, "my friends and I will stay away from the bad ones!"

The 1950 United States census classified the people of Puerto Rico as 79.7 per cent white and 20.3 per cent non-white. The proportion of non-whites has been dropping steadily since the 38.6 per cent found in the first United States census taken on the island in 1899. This is one of the many indications of peaceful relationships between the two races.

When he comes to the States, the Puerto Rican newcomer who is colored may experience his first difficulty getting a job or finding a place to live because of his color. Naturally, he will be puzzled and frustrated. More important, he may find his self-esteem reduced by two possible, perhaps simultaneous, demotions. First, instead of a dignified human being with full social rights he has become a member of a minority group. Second, he may be further relegated to the position of being a minority within a minority, a Negro within the Puerto Rican group. Census figures show that fewer non-white Puerto Ricans come to the States than whites, in comparison with their proportion of the population, and a special study indicates that a larger percentage of the non-whites return to their original homes after a sojourn on the mainland. The 1960 census found 3.9 per cent of the persons of Puerto Rican birth living in the U.S. to be non-white.

Furthermore, the Negro often misunderstands the fact that the dark or even black Puerto Rican does not react as the Negro expects him to react. There is no need in Puerto Rico for separate "defense" or "civil rights" organizations for the darker people—and none exists. Puerto Rican attitudes do not change quickly; the pressure toward conformity with the prejudices of the receiving society are widely resisted. The statement presented at New York City Board of Education hearings on integration, on behalf of the Puerto Rican Forum, said ". . . the Puerto Rican looks at himself as being wholly integrated racially. He rejects the notion that he has to seek out white or Negro classmates where within his own culture you find the full range from rosy pink to ebony black." Dr. Francisco Trilla, chairman of the Forum, was misunderstood by the Negroes when he stated: "We would rather be considered as members of the human race and forget the racial denotations." A carefully reasoned statement by Joseph Monserrat, director of the Migration Division of the Puerto Rico Department of Labor, at an integration conference at Teachers' College, Columbia University, pointed out that ". . . an all Puerto Rican school may well be, from a 'racial' point of view, the most integrated of schools." He pointed out that it was cultural differences which were crucial. He hit at the increasingly popular cliché of the "culturally deprived child," as applied to the Puerto Rican pupil, in the following question:

> Is a culture that has for four centuries been able to maintain the individual dignity, value and worth of its members (despite differences in race and class) a deprived or disadvantaged culture when compared with one that has been striving to achieve these values and has yet not been able to do so?

Negro reactions range from understanding acceptance to outright hostility. The Youth Conference of the NAACP a few years ago demanded that migration from Puerto Rico be stopped. A Harlem group in June, 1964, asked that Puerto Ricans on certain jobs be discharged so that Negroes could be hired. These actions were repudiated by Negro leaders, but the *Newsweek* survey in 1963 showed more puzzlement than either approval or disapproval of Puerto Ricans by both leaders and rank and file.

The Negro sample was asked to assess the role played by certain non-Negro religious and ethnic groups in "the Negro revolution." Catholic priests and Jews were both rated high as being helpful. White churches, in general, were not found very helpful, but the answers in regard to the Puerto Ricans were overwhelmingly "not sure"; 75 per cent of the rank and file and 69 per cent of the leaders gave that answer.

The reasons are probably a compound of what to the Negro seems to be an avoidance of obviously the most important question in the world, plus the relative success of the Puerto Rican in retail businesses in Negro neighborhoods. A Negro poet, Claude McKay, pointed out in 1940 that "Today 99 per cent of the community's [Harlem's] commerce is done by Puerto Ricans and other members of the Spanish-speaking colonies."

The Negro leaders are twice as likely as the rank and file to rate the Puerto Ricans as "helpful." They are, first, more likely to understand the cultural factors involved and, second, probably more aware of the role the dark-skinned Puerto Rican often plays in helping with the desegregation of "lily white" places of employment and neighborhoods. The very fact that the black man may be labeled "Puerto Rican" has been helpful in giving him a chance at a job. This is often followed by employment of Negroes without the convenient label. "Ain't semantics wonderful," one of the author's friends remarked!

Skin color affects the geographical mobility of the Puerto Rican here. A Columbia University study conducted in 1948 found a substantial difference between East Harlem, where 57 per cent of the Puerto Rican population was white, and the Morrisania area of the Bronx, where 77 per cent was white. If the study had been carried out among the more economically successful Puerto Ricans who are scattered through Washington Heights, Inwood, Queens, Yonkers, and the New Jersey and Long Island suburbs, the percentage of white would have been still higher. What this proves, of course, is that dark-complexioned people of any origin have difficulties when they try to move out of distinctive "colored" neighborhoods.

Subsistence and Assistance

The professional xenophobe quoted earlier made much of the idea that Puerto Ricans came to the States to go on relief and that a majority are on relief rolls. Many serious-minded citizens have become concerned about these charges even though both have been refuted a number of times. The Columbia University study found that 6 per cent were on relief in the winter of 1947-48. About two years later, a Welfare Department report indicated that the proportion was about 10 per cent. Unemployment in New York City had increased from about 170,000 in the earlier period to around 250,000 in the later one (as measured by those registered for unemployment insurance payments). Naturally, the Puerto Rican newcomer who is the "last to be hired" is "the first to be fired." Like migration, the number on relief is governed by the ups and downs of the business cycle; and this is true of all workers throughout the nation, irrespective of ethnic group. In addition to the latest arrivals, unskilled workers of any color or ethnic origin are always the most vulnerable to recessions.

The welfare picture in mid-1963 showed that 4.5 per cent of the country's big city population was receiving some form of public assistance—old-age pensions, aid to dependent children, aid to the blind, aid to the disabled, or home relief. New York City was just below the national average.

Minority groups were, of course, found more often in the lists of those having to resort to such means of living. *The New York Times* reported on June 2, 1957, that "about 11 per cent of the city's Puerto Ricans and 10 per cent of its Negroes may be on relief. A considerable number are fully self-supporting, while many others receive 'supplementation' relief only, to fill out inadequate earnings." Figures for 1964 from the Welfare Department indicate that about 20 per cent of the Negroes and Puerto Ricans were on relief. The hospital strike in 1959 dramatized the fact that the city was supporting the hospitals indirectly by paying many of their workers the difference between the below-subsistence wages they received and the cost of subsistence in New York City. A New York City Welfare Department study in August, 1959, showed that 51.7 per cent of all Puerto Ricans on relief were employed but not earning enough to support their families; they were therefore receiving supplementary relief. The proportion for the Negroes was 43 per cent; for others 20 per cent.

In 1956, the Department of Welfare made a study of persons receiving non-resident public assistance in order to determine how long they had lived in the state before securing relief. The findings showed that such persons from Puerto Rico were the last to request public assistance; they had lived in the state, on the average, 5.4 months prior to receiving assistance. Persons from the South were second, with 4.4 months of residency. First to go on relief, after 4.2 months, were persons from all other states.

A similar study in August, 1959, found that 56 per cent of all relief cases had lived in the city for more than ten years before applying for relief; that 91.7 per cent had lived there for over one year. The remainder were split almost evenly between those with less than six months' (4.3 per cent) and those with over six months' (4.0 per cent) residence.

Two other facts about relief should be noted here. A December,

1961, review noted that only 2 per cent of all persons on relief were employable; this is not generally understood. Another fact is that the proportion of the New York City expense budget going to welfare had dropped from 15.7 per cent in 1950-51 to 11.6 per cent in 1961-62. In 1940 it was about 30 per cent.

THE "DELINQUENT" STEREOTYPE

Crime and juvenile delinquency are also favorite themes for the xenophobe and are, of course, matters of concern to every civic-minded person. Data are scanty with which to assess the rumors which involve Puerto Ricans in an inordinately large percentage of contemporary crime. What data there are do not support the stereotype. First, it should be noted that there was a substantial increase in crimes reported during and following World War II, just as there had been during and after World War I. If crimes were increasing everywhere, why should New York City be immune, and why, especially, should its most disadvantaged citizens—the "visible" minorities—be immune? Actually, the reports that do exist show the Puerto Rican just about at his "quota." *Time* (June 23, 1958) carried what is obviously an estimate derived from official sources: "Puerto Ricans form 8 per cent of the population and their share of the crime rate is only slightly more than 8 per cent."

One of the most telling illustrations of the damage which is done by the thoughtless use of statistics is contained in the 20th Annual Report of the Children's Court of New York City. It declared that "27 per cent of all the children who came to our court in Manhattan last year as delinquents were the children of Puerto Rican migrant parents, a figure out of all proportion, since the ratio of Puerto Rican-born citizens to the total city population is about 5 per cent."

It continued with the following sympathetic analysis of the situation:

The relatively large number of cases involving children of Puerto Rican parents could be ascribed to crowded, unsanitary living quarters and unfamiliarity with the English language, the report said.

"We believe, however," it added, "that the social difficulties inherent in this particular migration will not be long-lived but will yield to the constructive planning of the Government of Puerto Rico and the native pluck of these migrants."

Nonetheless, the stereotype of high delinquency among the Puerto Ricans was enormously reinforced by the headlines which played up the comparative figures. However, it was soon pointed out that several grave errors had been allowed to slip into the handling of the data. First, a legitimate comparison cannot be made between a percentage of juvenile delinquents and a percentage of the total population. Obviously, not everyone can become a juvenile delinquent; only juveniles can! Second, the comparison was being made between the experience of juveniles in Manhattan and the total Puerto Rican population. When a comparison was made between the proportion of the Manhattan juvenile population which was Puerto Rican (25 per cent) and the proportion given in the court's report (27 per cent), it was seen that the Puerto Rican juvenile was 2 percentage points above his "quota."

More recent reports from Children's Courts of all five boroughs of the city are consistent with the experience just cited. They state that 20 to 22 per cent of their clients, who are seven to fifteen years old, are of Puerto Rican birth or parentage. These ages are almost exactly equivalent to those of elementary and junior high school pupils. The Puerto Rican proportion of these two school levels has been running around 17 to 19 per cent in recent years.

The only fairly full study of Puerto Rican vs. non-Puerto Rican boys sentenced for juvenile delinquency shows a slightly higher percentage of delinquencies on the part of New York City-born Puerto Rican boys than for those born in Puerto Rico, and comes to the following conclusion:

> Puerto Rican delinquency, on the whole, is of a milder type. Ungovernability, home desertions, truancy, and other comparatively minor manifestations of maladjustment in the home or in the school are prevalent. Burglary and gang activities, involving felonious assault and homicide, are much less frequent than with the non-Puerto Ricans. Qualitatively speaking, the Puerto Rican boy in New York City does not present a serious delinquency problem.

Since this was written, however, there have been reports from the New York City Youth Board of increased gang activity involving Puerto Ricans. Harrison Salisbury of *The New York Times* points out the pervasive fear of adolescents living in slum areas which leads them to form gangs in self-defense.

This reminds one again of Jacob Riis, writing almost 70 years ago: "The gangs are an institution in New York . . . the ripe fruit of tenement house growth . . . gangs are made up of the American born of English, Irish, and German parents." But, as Salisbury points out, gangs are found throughout the world. They are even beginning to appear in San Juan as it grows in size and complexity, although gangs had been unknown there until a few years ago. Some are inclined to blame young people returning from New York City with bad habits!

While gang formation is a defensive reaction to an environment defined as hostile, the retreatist attitude is found in the use of narcotics. This seems to be on the increase among the Puerto Rican slum-dweller, although no data are available on the extent of such escapism.

A 1955 broad-scale study of Puerto Rican children in New York City schools found that in two Harlem school districts which were studied intensively, the court appearances for Puerto Rican children ran 12 per 1,000 pupils compared with 14 per 1,000 for non-Puerto Ricans. The Puerto Rican children represented 35 per cent of all pupils and 32 per cent of the referrals. They were below their proportion in sex delinquency, neglect, hold-ups, assault, gang fights, and incorrigibility; above in thefts, runaways, burglary, "marriage applications," and narcotics; and about equal in carrying weapons (mostly knives).

Some flavor of the difficulties facing the young Puerto Rican in "adjusting" to his new environment is given by a court case tried a few years ago. The judge was berating a Puerto Rican mother for not having made her teen-age son "get a good, decent American haircut instead of wearing those Puerto Rican sideburns." The mother sobbed her explanation that the boy had always cut his hair short in Puerto Rico but that since "the American boys now all want to act, talk and dress like Elvis Presley," she couldn't keep her son from wearing sideburns!

This ridiculous instance of ethnocentrism is, of course, an illustration of "second-generationitis." The conflict between the old culture and the new, between "old-fogey" parents and "modern" youth, has plagued our country (and others with large-scale internal migration or international immigration) for centuries. The children pick up new values, new ideas, new language, new habits and soon build up a new network of expectations. These are often at variance with those of the parents and may help increase the stresses and strains on the family. These in turn may have undesirable effects on mental health, as studies of this aspect of the lives of our ancestors and of various streams of internal migrants have shown.

Are the Puerto Ricans following our ancestors in coming to terms with their new environment? One of New York's great social workers, Miss Maryal Knox, when she was given a farewell banquet upon retirement, gave an answer based on her 50 years of work in the settlement house movement.

She said she was encouraged by the fact that her Puerto Rican neighbors "are being assimilated into the life of the city faster than any previous group, partly through their own impressive efforts and partly because we're learning better how to help the process."

Chapter 5
OURSELVES AS NEIGHBORS

WE" have improved considerably in our thinking about human beings who do not belong to our particular ethnic or racial group. Our actions still lag behind our knowledge, but we have made significant strides forward in our actions. These advances have made the integration process somewhat easier for the newest "strangers," as Miss Maryal Knox indicated.

Where have we improved and what do we still need to do?

Generally, we are beginning to apply the concepts and methods of science in our relations with others. Perhaps we will never achieve complete objectivity, but if all of us applied a healthy degree of caution when we discuss other people, a great deal of harm could be eliminated.

We have progressed in our thinking perhaps furthest by ruling out "inherent racial tendencies" as an explanation for the conduct of allegedly "inferior" or "superior" groups. No student of human affairs today, with the exception of a few of those isolated in backward areas, believes in the myth of inherently "inferior" or "superior" races or ethnic groups. Social scientists have shown it to be as completely without foundation as it was in the eleventh century when Saïd of Toledo, a Moorish savant, warned his listeners that:

> Races north of the Pyrenees are of cold temperament and never reach maturity; they are of great stature and of a whiter color. But they lack all sharpness of wit and penetration of intellect.

Those interested in maintaining the institution of slavery had many "scientific" arguments (as well as "religious" ones) to salve the consciences of the slaveholders. All have fallen into the ashcan of history along with other beliefs which at one time were the absolute truths against which it was dangerous to contend—such as that the sun rotates around the earth or that the earth is flat.

There are some corollaries which belong in the same ashcan but have not yet been completely discarded: e.g., that some racial groups are "temperamentally" different from others, that there are racial differences in disease and death rates independent of social, economic, and geographic conditions, and that cultural differences, including morals, are actually racial differences. These are all expressions of ethnocentrism, of the belief that one's own group has the only correct solution to ways of working, living, playing, and praying.

One of the most harmful ideas, because presumably "scientific," is that some groups are inherently more intelligent than others. There has been almost complete consensus for several decades among scientists that there is no evidence supporting this viewpoint. Among many who could be cited is C. C. Brigham: ". . . This review has summarized some of the more recent text findings which show that comparative studies of various national and racial groups may not be made with existing tests, and which show, in particular, that one of the most pretentious of these comparative racial studies —the writer's own—was without foundation." Twenty years later, after a number of attempts to develop better "intelligence" tests, one of the great psychologists, Dr. Florence Goodenough, wrote in 1950, "The search for a culture-free test, whether of intelligence, artistic ability, personal-social characteristics, or any other measurable trait, is illusory . . . my earlier study is certainly no exception to the rule . . . the writer hereby apologizes for it." A recent symposium edited by Professor Melvin Tumin of Princeton University dealt with a recrudescence of racist literature (some of it financed by the governor of Alabama). The vice president of the Educational Testing Service indicates that the present-day opinion of authorities in the field still upholds the Bingham and Goodenough statements. He states flatly that "the nature of intelligence tests is such that they are incapable of identifying *native* (i.e., genetic) differences between any two groups, if indeed such genetic differences exist." He is joined in his approach by a Princeton psychologist, the chairman of the U.C.L.A. department of sociology and anthropology, and a past president of the American Anthropological Society.

We now know that race refers exclusively to physical features—skin color, hair texture, etc.—and has no relevance, as such, in human behavior. What makes it relevant is our *attitude* toward it!

In other words, there are no *human* problems which can properly be labeled "racial." We know that man's behavior, with the exception of his food and sexual appetites, is *learned* behavior. Even the social expression of his animal drives is governed by what his social environment has taught him.

Children of one race do not "naturally" hate children of another race. Children only hate those whom their environment teaches them to hate. In Liverpool, England, for example, the author found white children playing with Negro children with no friction whatever. The teachers told him, however, that the same children wouldn't play with "lower class" white children!

We have learned what a terrible toll discrimination takes, not only from those who suffer from it, but from those who exercise it and from the nation as a whole. Elmo Roper, as both a businessman and one of the country's outstanding research practitioners, estimates that discrimination costs us $30 billion every year in lost manpower and productivity.

Immigrants Are History

We have also learned to view our history as the story of strangers becoming neighbors. The great historian Oscar Handlin won the Pulitzer Prize for his book *The Uprooted,* in which he says: "Once I thought to write a history of the immigrants in America. Then I discovered that the immigrants *were* American history." The widespread recognition of Handlin's prize-winning book is encouraging evidence of our improvement.

Another perceptive, as well as witty, glimpse at the past, which fortunately has had a phenomenal sale, is the warm and winning book, *Only in America,* by Harry Golden. Golden's essay, "A Short Story of America," only a portion of which can be cited here, is a gem. The scene is the main reading room of the New York Public Library which Golden always visits on his trips to New York.

Numbers flashed on the ground glass indicator to signify books ready for pick-up. Golden stayed long after his own number was flashed. He was, he writes, ". . . watching the whole story of America. A whole course in sociology within a half-hour. I saw boys and girls go up to pick up their books. Many of them were Puerto Rican boys and girls, stepping up to the indicator desk and getting their books and I thought how 'bad' news is really 'good' news. We read of the delinquency and the crime—but this is the real answer. It is that people are people, and they reflect the environment and the conditions which surround them. In my day it was Jewish boys and girls who stepped up to that indicator counter. Jewish boys and girls, many of them still wearing the clothes their mothers had made for them for the trip across the ocean. And before the Jewish boys, the Irish boys and girls picked up their books and after the Jewish boys and girls, the Italians did the same thing, and then the Negroes, and now the Puerto Ricans. And what is going on with the Puerto Ricans is exactly what went on with all the others. The Irish 'West Side Dusters' and 'Hell's Kitchen' gangs and the Jewish 'Lefty Loueys' and 'Gyp the Bloods' and the Italian 'Dago Franks' and Mafia, and now the Puerto Rican delinquents, and dope peddlers—all these made the headlines, but America was made in that library, and these same people helped make it."

"The Old Tenement Trail" is the title Samuel Lubell, the political analyst, gives to his account of what happened to the people of Rivington Street in the Lower East Side of Manhattan who were referred to in 1911 as "sickly faced immortal creatures who lie closer than any wild animal would lie." Lubell follows several "tenement house trails," one of which leads him to Queens: "Here today," he writes, "will be found many of the 'sickly faced immortal creatures' . . . But how they have changed! Because they spent their youth in rootless tenements which knew no community life, they have been buying homes and have become doubly civic-minded in their eagerness to build a community in which their children might escape the deprivations of their own childhood. From Rivington Street to Forest Hills in Queens is only a few miles. Historically, the spanning of that distance was a social revolution."

The same process of social exploration can be demonstrated with any minority element in all of our larger cities. By going up and down the ladder of neighborhoods through which different elements have climbed, one can see the progress they have made and the setbacks they have suffered—their clashes and reconciliations with other ethnic elements, and their integration into American society generally.

Our understanding of what happened in the slums of the past

is reinforced by contemporary studies. Frederick M. Thrasher, as a result of extensive investigations into crime and delinquency, concludes that ". . . the children of immigrants do not form gangs more readily than the native-born of native stock living under similar conditions; the difference is primarily due to the fact that the latter live less frequently in gang-breeding areas."

The Influence of the Slum

The slum is the villain then—not its inhabitants. Thrasher continues: "Further important evidence along the same line is the fact that the rates of delinquency for urban immigrant areas tend to remain unchanged and consistently high in spite of the fact that a succession of different immigrant groups occupies the same district over a long period of years. As a result of careful statistical studies in Chicago, [Clifford] Shaw states the illuminating conclusion that: 'The racial and nationality composition of the population in these areas of high rates of delinquents changed almost completely between 1900 and 1920, while the relative rates of delinquents remain practically unchanged.' Furthermore, the delinquency rates of the children and immigrant parents in delinquency areas show a decline when the families move to better neighborhoods. Again Shaw concludes: 'As the older immigrant groups moved out of the areas of high rates of delinquency, the rates of delinquency among the children of these groups decreased and they tended to disappear from the juvenile court.' "

We are beginning to get a better conception than we had when these data were first collected and analyzed as to *why* the slum environment produces more entries on the police blotter than those of other areas in the city. "Poverty" at one time was the answer, but the truth is that, on the one hand, only a minority of the poor people of the slums ever get into trouble with the police and, on the other, there are many middle- and upper-class crimes and delinquencies. "Depraved and perverse" individuals were also once blamed, but we now know that criminals and delinquents do not conform to any *type* such as César Lombroso and others once believed, just as we know that no one ethnic group "naturally" produces more law-breakers than another.

At one time it was thought that a "low I.Q." brought on crime and delinquency. Now, however, we realize that differences in intelligence test scores are largely a reflection of class or other group differences in the rearing of a child, especially the duration and quality of his education. His culture, meaning what his group taught him to believe to be right and wrong, also influences his attitude toward school. And his culture's concept of time may significantly affect the results on tests which often are given with stop-watch in hand.

The Influence of the Group

Almost all of us are overwhelmingly influenced by what the groups we belong to—or would like to belong to—expect of us. But what happens if we belong to groups with different and conflicting requirements? What happens if the group we would like to be a part of rejects us? What happens if the group that accepts us most readily and gives us the greatest sense of satisfaction turns out to be a group which is at war with conventionally organized society? This is the type of question that will get us closer to an understanding of what happens to individuals who get into trouble.

The Berkshire International Forum on Delinquency, in June 1951, asserted that "the roots of delinquent behavior lie in part in the defects of society itself." We are all required to "adjust" to society, but to which "pattern" of society do we adjust?

Where is the stranger—no matter of what ethnic group—to find acceptance, to find security, to find a chance to feel that he can "let his guard down," to find not only models of behavior, but a *chance* to behave in the way the new group expects him to, and to be rewarded as if he were a member of the group toward which he would orient his life? An individual cut off from his fellows, unwanted, unloved, deprecated, and rejected, is a person without moorings, liable to drift with whatever tide sweeps his way. A *group* which is similarly rejected will either disintegrate or huddle together for protection and develop its own attitudes and values, which may or may not be those of the dominant society.

Large numbers of our ancestors were placed in such a position by the "melting pot" school of "Americanizers" and by other forms of rejection. Those who urged that the immigrant "forget the past" were asking the impossible—at least the undesirable.

Strangers in a new land will fit in better with the society around them as they gain opportunities to participate in that society. This means providing them with greater economic opportunity and giving them greater responsibility to guide their own destinies.

We have learned enough about the way people are influenced by social situations to know that society offers the young of both older inhabitants and newcomers contradictory patterns and models. They want to follow the rules but they are confronted with "big shots" in various fields who saw the "main chance" and grabbed it—even though they had been taught that such action wasn't ethical. An outstanding movie actress who got her real start in life by posing for "overexposed" photographs justified her actions in an interview (illustrated) in a national magazine by saying, "If I'd observed all the rules, I'd never have got anywhere." Why should an attractive dime-store clerk think she may not be similarly rewarded for breaking the rules? Or the youngster who has been taught that wealth and power are the major sources of the social status he needs, particularly if he comes from an underprivileged group?

Health—Mental and Physical

Insecurity and competition are found by social scientists and psychiatrists to be damaging to the personality. The psychiatrist Karen Horney points out that "from its economic center competition radiates into all other activities and permeates love, social relations, and play. Therefore, competition is a problem for everyone in our culture, and it is not at all surprising to find it an unfailing center of neurotic conflicts."

We know that disadvantaged persons suffer more from both infectious and chronic diseases, although these formerly were considered exclusively in individual terms. The Secretary-General of Great Britain's National Association for the Prevention of Tuberculosis, Dr. Harley Williams, a few years ago gave one of the clearest explanations of the modern view of therapy. He declared that tuberculosis patients die not only from the effects of the disease-causing germ but also "from inward despair which lowers their resistance and prevents their taking advantage of the help the community is able to offer." With all the recent medical advances in the treatment of tuberculosis "there is danger we are getting too much science and too little understanding," he asserted. The germ which causes tuberculosis, Dr. Williams continued, "is really only one-half the cause. The other half lies in unhealthy social conditions, bad nutrition, and in personal anxiety and strain of body and mind. Most of the scientific methods are directed against the germ. Their very success may tempt us to ignore the patient's background and the patient's own psychology."

Dr. Williams' warnings are reinforced by recent studies in this country showing that medical staffs, even in such sensitive areas of practice as psychotherapy, are influenced by the bias arising out of their middle-class background. One report shows that higher-status patients more frequently receive psychotherapy than those of lower status, who are more likely to receive organic treatment, "shock" treatments, or no therapy; and that social status is closely related to acceptance of therapy, length of therapy, duration of therapy sessions, and choice of therapist. They also found that while therapists "liked" nine out of thirteen higher-class patients, they "disliked" nine out of twelve lower-class patients; and that while only six of the higher-class patients were rated as having poor communication with the therapist, all the lower-class patients were so rated.

We have learned two lessons about health. First, health is a purchasable commodity—i.e., if the community wants to eradicate most diseases, it can do so. This is now one of the cornerstones of the preventive health movement. The second, and just as important, as is shown by Dr. Williams and many others, is a lesson which it seems difficult for us to learn—dollars are not enough. The same two lessons are applicable to the prevention of juvenile delinquency and other expressions of social and personal disorganization.

"Cultural Democracy"

Does our increased knowledge lead to increased action? One is reminded of that great spirit of the social settlements, Paul U. Kellogg, complaining that, "We run the risk of being the best informed and most inhibited democracy in the world." The pioneer settlement houses—Henry Street and Greenwich House in New York, and Hull House in Chicago, for example—fought for the enforcement of tenement house laws, for slum clearance, for more and better schools, for more parks and playgrounds. They fought for recognition by the community of the immigrants' right to be treated as human beings, to dignity, to be "different" and not to suffer from it. It is encouraging to note that the constantly refined tools of social research are proving what Jane Addams, Lillian Wald, Paul U. Kellogg, Mary Simkhovitch, and others knew from their experience and their deep understanding of the well springs of human behavior. They worked out the goal which has only recently been labeled "cultural democracy," one of the most magnificent concepts formulated in the history of the human race.

The settlements are still struggling to help solve the difficulties arising from the major transition now taking place in our cities. Most of the newcomers today are citizens, but they come from areas where behavior patterns are not those of the big-city dweller. Urban behavior is learned behavior and must be taught—whether it is taught over the years to the child who grows up in the city or is taught under pressure to the newcomer. Often it is the overtones of such teaching which give rise to difficulties in communication between the individuals and institutions of the receiving community and the newcomer. In other words, good human relations are basic to the teaching process.

A tremendous increase of interest in and activity on behalf of better relations between persons of different colors, creeds, and national origins has marked the past three decades in the United States. Two major trends can be traced within the programs of both official and private voluntary agencies. One is the acceptance of "cultural democracy," or "cultural pluralism," as contrasted with the formerly dominant "melting pot" approach to persons who are not included among the "WASPS" (white Anglo-Saxon Protestants). Sometimes this approach is called, by analogy, "orchestration," or "tapestration." It implies that "unity with diversity" is the ideal of the democratic citizen of the United States, that just as violins or colorful threads make their contribution to a symphony or a tapestry, so the "strangers in a strange land" need not divest themselves of their culture heritage.

Dean E. George Payne of New York University points out the role of education in building cultural democracy:

> If the cultural pluralism theory is correct, then the problem of adjustment becomes essentially that of preserving cultural traits, of dignifying qualities and practices different from our own, and of creating a feeling of pride in the folkways, mores, customs, conventions, and social patterns, characteristic of the immigrant in his homeland as well as of the Negro and the Indian. Education, there-

fore, under this theory assumes a totally different role. It begins by discovering their characteristics, by magnifying them, by dignifying them, and by creating a feeling of pride in them.

Education, however, does not end here, but continues by building into the original cultural patterns the best of American traditions, so that the growth and development of the minority groups may be continuous and effective.

The only other option is cultural deterioration, the disintegration of family life, and maladjustment in our social life.

The Organizational Approach

The second major trend in the programs of official and private agencies has been toward a generic approach to problems of what were formerly known as "race relations." It is now increasingly realized that "Negro-white relations are not fundamentally different from the minority-dominant group relations involving Catholics, Jews, Spanish-Americans, and Japanese-Americans."

Organizations working to advance the cause of better relations between various ethnic and religious groups have been growing rapidly in numbers and in personnel, in budget and in public influence in recent years. Professional workers in the field formed a nationwide organization in 1946—the National Association of Intergroup Relations Officials. Its membership in 1964 consisted of some 1,200 professional members compared with 287 seven years before.

Almost all Catholic, Jewish, and Protestant church bodies now carry out specialized programs in the human relations field. The largest of all the voluntary agencies in the field is the interfaith organization called the National Conference of Christians and Jews. One of its major contributions in recent years has been the organization of institutes on police-community relations in the interest of a better understanding of community dynamics on the part of the guardians of law and order. It is through them that the stranger often has his first contact with the institutional structure of his new community.

Often misunderstandings lead to puzzlement, irritation, and frustration on the part of both newcomers and police—sometimes resulting in hostile actions on both sides. A police seminar in Puerto Rico for 57 officers from 38 localities in the United States with sizable Puerto Rican populations cleared up, for example, the question of "loitering" on the sidewalk. First, there is no anti-loitering law in Puerto Rico. The mainland police were incredulous when told by their Puerto Rican colleagues that groups always broke up and went home if they were asked politely! Second, it was found that part of the adverse reaction which sometimes was aroused when a policeman told a group that if they didn't break up they would be arrested for "loitering" came from the similarity between that word and "lotería"—meaning here the "numbers" game!

There are instances in too many cities where Puerto Ricans and other minority groups are subjected to brutal handling by the police. U.S. Civil Rights Commission records are, unfortunately, replete with cases. On the other hand, a number of police institutes are now giving courses in Spanish to help both sides avoid problems.

Obviously, public opinion must be prepared for integration in housing as well as in employment, schools, places of amusement, restaurants, transportation, and other public services. An enormous amount of research has been done in the field of neighborhood change. It indicates, overwhelmingly, that most rumors and fears about property values being endangered by minority group neighbors are not well founded. It is fear itself which usually does the damage. In some cities, frequently through the leadership of local ministers and their parishioners, neighborhoods have successfully prevented the "scare selling" of homes through the erection of such signs as: "This home *not* for sale. I believe in my community and my neighbor."

In 1958 the private Commission on Race and Housing issued an impressive report called *Where Shall We Live?* This continues to be an important resource for the civic-minded, as are the five reports which have been published by the University of California Press. An extremely helpful *Guide to Changing Neighborhoods* is available from the National Community Relations Advisory Council, made up of six national Jewish organizations and 38 local Jewish groups. The *Freedom Pamphlets* of the Anti-Defamation League, the National Labor Service of the American Jewish Committee, the Commission on Law and Social Action of the American Jewish Congress, and the Labor Reports of the Jewish Labor Committee —all these indicate the tremendous activity of Jewish groups in this area.

The newness of Puerto Rico is reflected in this view of the Miramar section in San Juan.

A city project in Puerto Rico demonstrates the emphasis on modern, low-income housing.

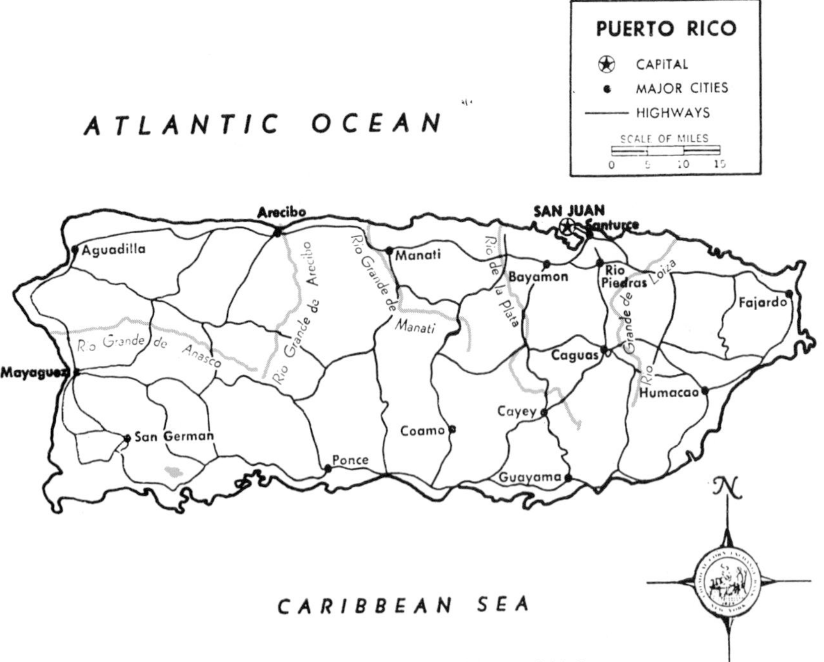

A general map of Puerto Rico showing major cities and highways.

A Puerto Rican sugar farmer and his family at their house on a medium-sized sugar "finca."

Self-help programs in Puerto Rico include housing construction.

An adult education class talks about management.

In Caguas, an elementary school student reads from an English reader.

An evening English course in New York City. Puerto Ricans are among 57 groups taking such courses.

A typical street scene in the Puerto Rican neighborhood of New York.

In New York's Puerto Rican colony, youngsters rarely have access to model playgrounds. *(Wide World Photo)*

The Spanish-speaking community of New York City, including Puerto Ricans, celebrates Columbus Day.

Church Programs

The Catholic Church, the Catholic Council for the Spanish-Speaking (in the Southwest), and the Catholic Inter-racial Councils work assiduously among their co-religionists. The National Council of Churches carries on a widespread program through several divisions: the Division of Home Missions handles farm migrants—Mexicans, Indians, Puerto Ricans, and other rural groups—while urban work is conducted through a Department of the Urban Church. There is also a special Committee on Spanish-American Work. The Council organized a conference at the Union Theological Seminary in Rio Piedras, Puerto Rico, in 1959 to work out exchanges of experience and personnel between Puerto Rico and the States. Individual denominations arrange special work—e.g., the Division of Racial Minorities of the National Council of the Episcopal Church held a conference on the Puerto Ricans in the United States. There is a great deal of cooperative activity between the eight major Protestant denominations in the Commonwealth and their brethren in this country.

The American Friends Service Committee carries on a widespread program of work with disadvantaged groups: Indians, Mexicans, and Puerto Ricans, among others. The Unitarian-Universalist Service Committee does similar work.

Local church groups have programs of varying scope. The Archdiocese of New York in 1953 created Spanish Catholic Action, and the Archbishop's Committee on the Spanish-Speaking in Chicago has been active for about the same length of time. The Catholic Church in the States is cooperating with the new Catholic University in Ponce, Puerto Rico, to help train priests and social workers for service to the newcomer. All the major religious organizations cooperated in the magnificent "March on Washington" in 1963.

City, State, and Federal Programs

National and local voluntary organizations have blazed the trail and helped in the creation of official city and state agencies to promote better human relations. Some of these depend entirely on education and, where necessary, conciliation. Prominent among them are the Mayor's Friendly Relations Committee of Cincinnati, the Chicago Commission on Human Relations, and similar groups in Philadelphia, Milwaukee, Newark, Lehigh County (Pennsylvania), and scores of other communities throughout the country.

New York State passed a law forbidding discrimination in hotels, inns, public conveyances, places of amusement, public schools, colleges, and cemeteries in 1874, but the predecessor of the present State Commission on Human Rights to aid in enforcing the law was not created until 1945. New York City, which did not desegregate its public schools until 1900, recently gave its Commission on Human Rights responsibility for enforcing its anti-discrimination law in housing, as well as in employment and public accommodations.

The federal Civil Rights Act of 1964, signed by President Johnson on July 2, is the keystone of an arch which has been painfully erected over the past 20 years. It included, during World War II, the Fair Employment Practices Act, which was a victim of the "return to normalcy." However, a Committee on Government Contracts has helped to insure that federal funds would not be used to purchase commodities in plants where job discrimination is practiced. Two presidential committees were appointed on equal opportunity in employment and in housing. The United States Commission on Civil Rights was created by congressional action in 1957 and has been most active in bringing to light violations of civil liberties and civil rights in employment, voting, housing, education, and in the administration of the law. Their public hearings and a constant stream of publications have helped the civil rights cause tremendously.

Chicago has created a specific organization to help newcomers find their way around the urban maze, the Mayor's Committee on New Residents of the Commission on Human Relations, formed in January, 1957. The preamble of the order creating it states:

> Chicago is historically a city of opportunity. Waves of immigrants have come to it seeking political freedom and economic opportunity, learning its language, adapting culture and habit to the demands of a strange industrial complex.
>
> The present migration differs in that most of these new residents are already United States citizens and a good many of them know the language. These new residents, however, have a rural background and are unfamiliar with the priorities of industry, the

demands of city living, the resources a city makes available to them, and the nearness of hundreds of thousands of other people who apparently know their way around.

The committee identifies the six major groups to which the newcomers will belong as American Indians, European immigrants, Mexicans, Puerto Ricans, Southern Negroes, and Southern whites. Puerto Rican migration is characterized by the influence of the business cycle, already mentioned; the Southern white by a seasonal trek to the South when cold weather begins and a return to the North with spring.

There are also specialized national organizations working in specific fields: the National Committee Against Discrimination in Housing, the National Association for the Advancement of Colored People, and the National Urban League, for example. The last was created in response to the northward, urban movement of Negroes just prior to World War I. New organizations have sprung into existence in the past few years as expressions of rapidly increasing demands for an application of democratic ideals to our Negro citizens. CORE (the Congress of Racial Equality); the Reverend Martin Luther King's Southern Christian Leadership Conference; and the Student Non-violent Coordinating Committee are among the most important of the newer groups. They are striving desperately to turn increasing Negro militancy into constructive channels but are being combatted bitterly by the racism of the White Citizens' Councils, the Ku Klux Klan, and the Black Muslims.

To one degree or another almost all the largest and most influential civic groups have now incorporated the improvement of inter-group relations into their programs, e.g., the Boy Scouts, the YM and YWCA's, and some service clubs.

Trade Union Interest

The AFL-CIO maintains a civil rights department which conducts conferences and issues literature describing the harmful effects of discrimination on working and living conditions and on labor organizations. Its Education Department issues material in Spanish. In 1952, New York City representatives of the AFL and the CIO helped organize a Committee on Puerto Rican Workers. It felt it must combat not only employers who stirred up animosity between Negroes and other ethnic groups and Puerto Ricans, but also racketeering unions which have made "sweetheart" agreements with equally unscrupulous employers for the joint exploitation of their workers' ignorance of prevailing wage rates.

The committee was reorganized in 1957 and was strengthened by the assignment of a full-time organizer by President George Meany. The name was changed to the Committee to End the Exploitation of Puerto Ricans and other Minority Groups.

The Community Services Committee of the AFL-CIO has run many local community leadership training institutes in which Puerto Rican and other minority group members have participated. It issues materials in Spanish. Nine international unions affiliated with the AFL-CIO now maintain headquarters in Puerto Rico; this gives all of them more interest in being helpful to the stranger at their doors in this country.

The International Ladies' Garment Workers' Union probably carries on more activities designed to incorporate the Spanish-speaking worker into its ranks than any other international. Many others, however, publish bilingual papers, conduct business meetings in two languages, organize English and other classes and social events for their new members, and issue union literature in languages other than English.

The ILGWU has a tradition of working with non-English-speaking members. For years it has published its official organ, *Justice,* in Yiddish, Spanish, and Italian editions. Its Local 600, in Puerto Rico, sends a big delegation to national conventions and is always given a rousing welcome. A 1957 research report on "Puerto Rican Integration in the Skirt Industry in New York City" begins with what undoubtedly is the consensus of both employers and labor officials:

> From the viewpoint of New York City's economic future, facilitating the entrance of Puerto Ricans into its industry is of vital importance. Their subsequent integration into trade unions is of equal importance to the future of New York's labor movement.

"Operation Rapport" was started in 1958. Labor union officials studied Puerto Rico and the Puerto Ricans in the local labor movement and then visited the island. It was conducted jointly by the Central Labor Council, the Commonwealth Department of Labor Migration Division, and the New York State Department of Labor. The educational program was worked out by Cornell

University's School of Industrial and Labor Relations and the Labor Relations Institute of the University of Puerto Rico. Two affiliates of the International Brotherhood of Electrical Workers have conducted similar study tours. Local 3, I.B.E.W. conducts large-scale recruitment among minority group members for its apprenticeship program. The Hotel Trades Council has created a Committee for Equal Opportunity and Promotion and has begun to organize members into neighborhood councils to combat exploitation by unscrupulous landlords and credit merchants.

Lois Gray estimates that there were some 70 Puerto Rican full-time union officials in New York City in 1963.

Changes in Attitude

Activity on behalf of better human relations seems to have made an impression, if one may judge by public opinion polls taken in 1942, 1956, and 1963. When the National Opinion Research Center, in 1942, asked a national cross-section of the population, "If a Negro family with the same income and education as you have moved into your block, would it make any difference to you?" 42 per cent of the Northerners and 12 per cent of the Southerners said it would not make any difference. When the same question was repeated in 1956, the proportion stating no objection to residential proximity had risen to 58 per cent in the North and 38 per cent in the South. By 1963, favorable replies in the North had risen to 70 per cent; in the South, to 51 per cent.

School integration was accepted by white Northerners on the following rising scale: 1952, 40 per cent; 1956, 61 per cent; and 1963, 75 per cent. White Southerners lagged behind: 1942, 2 per cent; 1956, 14 per cent; and 1963, 30 per cent.

Indicative of a fundamental change in racial attitudes, in both North and South, were replies in 1942, 1956, and 1963 to the question, "In general, do you think Negroes are as intelligent as white people—that is, can they learn things just as well if they are given the same education and training?" The proportion of white persons who believed Negroes equally intelligent rose in the North from 50 per cent to 80 per cent, and in the South from 21 per cent to 59 per cent.

People vary widely in the intensity of their prejudice toward minority groups. With allowance for shifts in the general level of prejudice and for regional differences, various studies support the conclusion that only a minor fraction of the population is strongly prejudiced. A small but growing fraction is strongly unprejudiced to the point of advocating racial equality. In between is the majority which is somewhat prejudiced but which does not feel strongly about racial issues one way or the other. This large group, with no strongly fixed opinions, is capable of being influenced by education or pressures from either side, according to the studies summarized by the Commission on Race and Housing.

The Hyman-Sheatley studies indicate that as the demand for civil rights becomes more insistent and persistent, the undecided group understands that it must choose sides in what Gunnar Myrdal called "the American dilemma": it is either democracy *or* racism. We cannot have it both ways.

Integration in the Schools

A milestone on the rough path to a more perfect democracy was the blow to discrimination struck by the U. S. Supreme Court on May 17, 1954, when it ruled that "separate but equal" is a contradiction in terms and must be replaced by a democratic approach to race relations in education.

Integration in neighborhoods will, of course, be reflected in integration in the schools, where it is essential that it be carried out if children are to learn to live together in peace and harmony. (The ADL pamphlet by William H. Kilpatrick, *Modern Education and Better Human Relations,* makes this abundantly clear and outlines a program showing how it can be achieved.) According to the *National Parent-Teacher* of October, 1958, Parent-Teacher Associations have been urged by their national organization to join in helping newcomers. It sounded the following call to action: "Every community should organize to meet the needs of the newcomers, so that they will be welcomed, guided, and counseled in the difficult task of establishing themselves. This is a project that the PTA might well undertake, realizing that these new families may be crucial to the future of the community. Offering them initial help is the way to enlist their long-term interest in programs for improving the community, the schools, and services for children." A local group, the United Parents Associations of New York, has held many special workshops on techniques to help bring Spanish-speaking parents into the organization.

New York City, with the largest Puerto Rican population, has naturally given a good deal of attention to helping speed up the integration process of these newcomers. There have been useful reports from: the Welfare Council (now the Community Council), the Association of Assistant Superintendents of Schools, Columbia University's Bureau of Applied Social Research, several settlement houses, the Public Education Association assisted by the New York University Research Center for Human Relations, the Institute of Physical Medicine and Rehabilitation of New York University-Bellevue Medical Center, the Protestant Council, the Brooklyn Council for Social Planning, the Manhattan Council of the Boy Scouts of America, the State Commission Against Discrimination, and others. Tremendous interest and enthusiasm have been shown by every level of officialdom, as well as by civic, religious, business, labor, and university leaders.

The Commonwealth of Puerto Rico, Department of Labor, through its Migration Division, has cooperated with the city in organizing three migration conferences in San Juan. These were held in 1953, 1955, and 1958. The Continuations Committee of the Third Conference reported in June, 1959, on the work which had been performed by the following city agencies: Commission on Intergroup Relations; Department of Correction; Board of Education; Fire Department; Department of Health; Department of Hospitals; Housing Authority; Department of Labor; Police Department; Department of Sanitation; Department of Welfare. It also gave a picture of the work of the Commonwealth, which will be covered in the next chapter.

Of course, the school system is the key to any large-scale educational effort in any society. New York's historians have not given adequate credit to the school teachers and administrators of the past in their heroic struggles to help the immigrants and their children. Nor can one adequately pay tribute to the work done by the present personnel of the Board of Education. The numbers of Puerto Rican children rose from 24,350 in 1947 to 179,223 in 1963. Puerto Rican pupils were enrolled, by the fall of 1963, in all but 4 per cent of the 588 elementary schools, in all but two of the 127 junior high schools, and in all of the 86 high schools.

Teacher and Home Visitor

One of the most valuable inventions to cope with a situation the schools haven't faced since the days of mass immigration is the combination teacher and home visitor. These are bilingual teachers who work with the classroom teacher during the day and visit the home during afternoons or evenings to follow up children who begin to display the results of culture conflict, of home overcrowding, of malnutrition, or any other difficulty. There are now 110 such teachers; they also aid in neighborhood community organization work, parents' activities, etc.

Summer workshops for teachers have been held in Puerto Rico each year since 1949. A "reverse workshop" of school personnel coming from Puerto Rico to New York City was begun in 1961, as was "Operation Understanding," which involves an interchange of 14 teachers for one year. One-week study visits to Puerto Rico for 50 principals of schools having concentrations of Puerto Rican pupils were begun in 1963. Special audio-visual aids have been prepared including a motion picture, *Bienvenidos.*

Spanish is now being taught in the 4th, 5th, and 6th grades; an experimental program of using Spanish as an auxiliary language in the teaching of science and mathematics is being conducted; after-school Spanish clubs exist in 30 elementary schools for those who wish to maintain or improve their mother tongue; and radio and television as well as 16 courses of regular classes are used for in-service training programs for teachers of English as a second language. Institutions of higher education including Brooklyn, Columbia, Hunter, Queens, and New York University are offering courses in such subjects as "the acculturation of the Puerto Rican child," and teaching English as a second language.

From 1953 to 1957 the Board of Education sponsored a special study under a grant-in-aid from the Ford Fund for the Advancement of Education. The 265-page report, issued in 1959, contains material which has been helpful and promises to be for years to come, both in New York City and elsewhere, in connection with Puerto Ricans or with other similarly disadvantaged groups. The report, plus teaching materials prepared by the Study, is being used under the direction of 121 special "coordinators" who function through workshops, inter-school visits, demonstration lessons, etc.

By no means is all of the work of the "non-English" coordinators with Puerto Rican children; the New York City system has large numbers of pupils entering each year speaking one of 30 different languages. Nor do all of the Spanish-speaking pupils come from Puerto Rico. Cuba, the Dominican Republic, Mexico, and most of the other Latin American countries are well represented.

The list of organizations helping people live in what is sometimes called the "asphalt jungle" of the metropolis could be continued: the Travelers Aid Association, created in 1917 to help the stranger, now has 106 local affiliates in the various states, plus one in the Commonwealth of Puerto Rico; there are Legal Aid societies in most of the larger cities to aid the stranger and the local poor people who become enmeshed in increasingly complicated legal machinery; the National Desertion Bureau strives to help the 6,000,000 persons in the country who are affected by desertions ("desertion is the poor man's divorce" as social workers have said for many decades); the Better Business Bureau helps protect the public against frauds in business which each year cheat the public of millions of dollars; an Institute on Fair Credit has been organized in Chicago by the Illinois Credit Union League and the Catholic Council on Working Life to help restrain "hoodwinking of migrants—Puerto Ricans, Mexicans, whites, and Negroes from rural regions in the South."

Problems to Be Solved

It is apparent we are doing a great deal. Much of what we do we *must* do just to maintain the necessities and amenities of metropolitan living, even if there were no migrants. We have not really faced the problems arising out of deep conflicts between those whose major interest is to make money out of human misery, degradation, and spoliation and those who genuinely want to live up to their ethical creeds and democratic teachings. We do not know how to control what *Fortune* magazine calls the "rapaciousness" of the owners of the slum dewellings. We do not quite know what to say to the landlady who wrote a New York daily complaining of overcrowding in her formerly "quiet and respectable" neighborhood: "At first I didn't want to rent them rooms but they [the Puerto Ricans] are paying so much I couldn't afford not to." We often forget that minorities are generally not allowed into a neighborhood until it is already well on the road to deterioration. The newcomer is forced to pay more than other prospective inhabitants. Then he becomes the symbol of the deterioration of the vicinity—and is blamed for it!

We have not yet conquered the desire for gain, harnessed to ethnocentrism, which produces in so many popular fiction magazines what has been called "unintentional" prejudice in the form of stereotyped descriptions of the majority "Anglo-Saxons" and of minority "foreigners" or Negroes. We have not yet made up our minds, despite the lessons of our history and the demonstrations by such economists as Theodore W. Schultz and Kenneth Galbraith, that greater investment in education is imperative.

We are still liable to apply the "double standard" to persons from groups other than our own, no matter who they may be. Sociologist Robert K. Merton has given us the classic statement on how in-group virtues are transformed into out-group vices. He contrasts the characteristics of Abraham Lincoln with those of two members of American "out-groups"—"Abe Cohen" and "Abe Korokawa":

> Did Lincoln work far into the night? This testifies that he was industrious, resolute, perseverant, and eager to realize his capacities to the full. Do the out-group Jews or Japanese keep these same hours? This only bears witness to their sweatshop mentality, their ruthless undercutting of American standards, their unfair competitive practices. Is the in-group hero frugal, thrifty, and sparing? Then the out-group villain is stingy, miserly, and penny-pinching. All honor is due the in-group Abe for his having been smart, shrewd, and intelligent, and, by the same token, all contempt is owing the out-group Abes for their being sharp, cunning, crafty, and too clever by far. Did the indomitable Lincoln refuse to remain content with a life of work with the hands? Did he prefer to make use of his brain? Then, all praise for his plucky climb up the shaky ladder of opportunity. But, of course, the eschewing of manual work for brain work among the merchants and lawyers of the out-group deserves nothing but censure for a parasitic way of life. Was Abe Lincoln eager to learn the accumulated wisdom of the ages by unending study? The trouble with the Jew is that he's a greasy grind, with his head always in a book, while decent people are going to a show or a ball game.

In historical perspective, however, we have advanced and we have been helpful to the newest of the newcomers. It may aid our understanding of the next chapter if we remember our history.

Here is another apt quotation from Harry Golden's "A Short Story of America":

> The immigrant needed to accelerate the process of integration, of proving his individual worth, of achieving self-esteem as quickly as possible. It was reflected after each of the great waves of immigration. Right after the Irish came, you had an era of Irish "excellence"—in sports, on the stage, in many of the creative arts.
>
> In those days no one heard of a Jewish baseball or football player. Those days belonged to the John L. Sullivans, and the Jim Corbetts, and the George M. Cohans, the John McCormacks, the Chauncey Olcotts, and the Victor Herberts. Then after the Irish came the Jews, and the same process was in full swing. The days of the settlement house and the introduction of basketball as a major American sport by Jewish immigrants. Those were the days of Benny Leonard, and Marshall Goldberg, and Benny Friedman, and Barney Ross, and Benny Bass, and Irving Berlin, and Fanny Brice, and George Gershwin. They in turn were followed by the Italians responding to the same "need"—to the same environment and to the same rewards. It was the day of DiMaggio, and Perry Como, and Yogi Berra, and Frank Sinatra, and Carmine DeSapio; and now we are entering upon the Negro era, responding to the same need, the same ideas and ideals. Your Irishmen on the playing field, and your Jews and Italians in the prize ring and on the concert stage are now making room for the Jackie Robinsons, the Willie Mayses, the Harry Belafontes, and the Pearl Baileys and as sure as this land endures, the day will one day belong to this new wave of poverty-stricken immigrants, the Puerto Ricans.
>
> In their day they will have judges, artists, ballplayers, prize fighters, and political leaders.

Chapter 6
THE PUERTO RICAN AS A NEIGHBOR

HARRY Golden's prediction is already coming true. Puerto Ricans have become prominent in several fields. There is José Ferrer of stage, screen, radio, and television; Jesus María Sanromá, Boston Symphony soloist and recording artist; Admiral Horacio Rivero, U.S.N.; Graciela Rivera, opera singer; Chita Rivera, Olga San Juan, Rita Moreno, and Juano Hernández, of screen fame; Tito Puente and Noro Morales, popular orchestra leaders; and Ruth Fernández, the great interpreter of Caribbean songs. Baseball fans will recognize such former and present major league names as Vic Power, Orlando Cepeda, Ruben Gomez, Jim Rivera, Luis Arroyo, Valmy Thomas, Félix Mantilla, Arnold Portocarrero, Juan Pizarro, and Roberto Clemente. One of the top professional golfers today is Juan Rodriguez. The world's junior welterweight boxing championship was captured in 1959 by Carlos Ortiz. The bantamweight championship was held by Sixto Escobar, also from Puerto Rico, from 1934 to 1940.

But these people are not our neighbors—not unless we happen to be movie or stage stars, artists, baseball players, or boxers! What about the man at the next workbench, the girl at the next desk, the family down the street? These are the Puerto Ricans Miss Maryal Knox was talking about; they are the ones she and so many others have referred to who are making a rapid adjustment. These are our Puerto Rican neighbors.

Let's find out what they're like. What were they doing in their old homes? What are they doing now? How are their lives in the United States different from the way they lived in Puerto Rico?

Puerto Rico as a Good Neighbor

First let's look at the Island itself. Recently it has become a "showcase of democracy"—an accomplishment of which both we and Puerto Ricans should be proud. *Life* magazine was so impressed with Puerto Rican development, with what it is doing to help the United States prove to the world that democracy holds real promise for the "underdeveloped" two-thirds of the world, that a few years ago it ran an editorial entitled "Thank Heaven for Puerto Rico."

Each year since 1950, about 1,900 persons from underdeveloped areas have traveled to Puerto Rico to learn the "hows" and "whys" of what Puerto Ricans call "Operation Bootstrap," but which has often been called "miracle in the Caribbean." Puerto Rico spends more than half a million dollars yearly to help its visitors find what they seek. It also operates under a contract with the International Cooperation Administration to help train technical assistance personnel from the United States for their work abroad.

Why has Puerto Rican economic and political development been called a "miracle"? How did this miracle occur? Of course, those who brought it about deny that it is a miracle at all. They point out that it took hard work, imagination, receptivity to new ideas, and a willingness to sacrifice immediate gains for future growth. It also took a governmental apparatus which is both efficient and honest.

Crucial as they are, governmental activities tell only part of the story. Puerto Rican citizens were themselves involved in working out their future. Without their eager cooperation, blueprints for social change would have gathered dust on the drafting board. Now, however, social progress can be seen statistically in health, education, degree of industrialization, per capita income, and many other areas. It can be seen, also, in the high state of *morale* of the people themselves.

Puerto Ricans realize that many problems remain. A favorite slogan is "jalda arriba," indicating an awareness of the "long, uphill pull." Let us see how far Puerto Rico has already traveled up the hill.

Colonialism was perhaps the first major obstacle to economic and political development. Spain ruled the island for four centuries, and although it left a rich cultural heritage, it did not leave much for the average citizen. It failed to establish a public school system (leaving 90 per cent of the population illiterate), and left behind it birth and death rates characteristic of an uneducated, poverty-stricken area and political machinery designed to serve outside interests. Resistance to Spanish rule became widespread, even at the community level. In 1898 there was a change of sovereignty.

Overwhelmingly, Puerto Ricans welcomed United States troops when we "freed" them, as well as the citizens of Cuba and the Philippines, from Spanish rule in 1898. We were not accustomed to running an empire, however, and we made many mistakes. It was not until the latter part of the 1930's that Puerto Rican citizens began sharing the responsibility of working out an extensive program of social, economic, and political reconstruction.

In 1917 citizenship was granted those Puerto Ricans who wanted it (only 288 out of 1,223,981 refused it), and the machinery of internal democracy was somewhat improved. No further real progress in this field was made until 1948, when Puerto Ricans elected their own governor for the first time in 450 years. By now it was obvious that colonial rule had deteriorated. But what kind of government would replace it? There were three alternatives presented in the 1948 elections: independence, which drew 65,351 votes; statehood, which received 182,977 votes; and the newly worked-out concept of "commonwealth," which received 392,386 votes, or 61.2 per cent of the total ballot.

The leading proponent of a Puerto Rican commonwealth was Luis Muñoz Marin, elected Governor in 1948, 1952, 1956, and 1960. The new arrangement was agreed to by the United States Congress in 1950, ratified by three separate votes of the Puerto Rican people, and incorporated into the Constitution of the Commonwealth of Puerto Rico, which was accepted by Congress and went into effect on July 25, 1952.

The preamble to the Constitution expresses the faith of the people in democracy as a form of government: "We understand that the democratic system of government is one in which the will of the people is the source of public power, the political order is subordinate to the rights of man, and the free participation of the citizen in collective decisions is assured."

The Constitution contains several unusual measures designed to aid the efficient functioning of a democracy. For example, under the Constitutional provisions guaranteeing minority-party representation, the majority party cannot make the almost 100 per cent clean sweep of seats in the legislature which single-member constituencies had made possible in the past. Today, the opposition has 26 seats in the legislature in spite of the fact that its share of the vote was only 10 percentage points higher in the 1964 election than when, prior to the Constitution, it had only three members.

U.N. Recognition

The United Nations Assembly voted, in November, 1953, by 26 to 16, to recognize that the Puerto Ricans had been "invested with the attributes of political sovereignty which clearly identify the state of self-government attained by the Puerto Rican people as an autonomous political entity." The Commonwealth had been recognized by the representatives of the world's peoples; the United States henceforth was not required to report to the U.N. each year on developments in one of its former "dependent areas." The commonwealth arrangement has been applauded as one of the great political inventions of our times. This is one reason the island is so frequently visited by people from colonial, semi-colonial, or recently liberated areas of the world. The transition from dependence to democracy was accomplished without damage to economic or social patterns.

Perfection of the Commonwealth Concept

The large majority of voters continue to back the concept of Commonwealth as the basis of a continuing and permanent relationship between Puerto Rico and the United States. There are, however, some cloudy aspects of the relationship as defined in 1952, which both the government party and its opponents wish to clear up.

Muñoz suggested on the tenth anniversary of the new status that a plebiscite be held in Puerto Rico offering a choice between (1) a perfected Commonwealth plan; (2) statehood; and (3) independence. Congress voted in June, 1964, for a joint commission to work out details of a new pact embodying a union with common citizenship, defense, currency, and free market, and arranging for a plebiscite. The powers of the federal government would be specifically defined and all others would be reserved to the people of Puerto Rico. President Johnson signed the bill in June, 1964. The commission consists of 13 members—seven from the federal government and six from the Commonwealth. All three major parties in Puerto Rico are represented.

It is hoped by many that a plebiscite on the three forms of status will reduce the enormous amount of time and energy now given to what many believe is a sterile debate. There is little indication, however, that either of the opposition parties will cease their agitation if they lose the referendum. Neither has any appreciable content to its platform and propaganda other than the status issue.

Muñoz surprised everyone in July, 1964, by refusing to run for the governorship. He does not wish to be regarded as "indispensable," nor does he wish to stand in the way of the development of newer, younger leadership. He also wants to devote the major portion of his time to political education, including the work of perfecting Commonwealth status. He was elected to the Puerto Rico Senate in November, 1964, and Roberto Sánchez Vilella was overwhelmingly elected governor.

"Operation Bootstrap"

"Operation Bootstrap" was launched as an effort to develop the people themselves as a major factor in raising levels of living: agricultural improvement and diversification, industrialization, greater education, and the knitting together of all these goals by coordinated planning have been the major programs.

Poverty, with all its attendant ills, is another part of the Puerto Rican heritage, as it is for three-fourths of the peoples of the world. Lack of resources, plus lack of imagination in using resources, have been heavy handicaps. Agricultural land is scarce on the mountainous island, where sub-tropical rains have eroded soil on hilly lands unmercifully. The Puerto Ricans can use only about one-half of an acre of land per person for farming, compared with about four acres in the mainland United States. Forest resources are practically nonexistent and no subsoil resources of any consequence have yet been found. Puerto Rico, in common with many of the developing areas of the world, suffers from a heavy population density and from a high birth rate. In 1960 each of the island's 3,435 square miles of area supported an average of 687 persons;

compared with 51 persons per square mile in the States. In other words, the economy of Puerto Rico has to support over 13 times the population per square mile that the rich and highly developed economy of the United States supports in its territory.

Agriculture had been dominated by sugar production with coffee and tobacco as secondary crops. The land now produces, in addition, pineapples, legumes, coconuts, avocados, sweet potatoes, and bananas. Cattle raising and dairying have become important sources of income. Many more persons are now landowners under agrarian programs than were two decades ago. The "500 Acre" law, on the books since 1900, has been enforced and land held illegally under it has been expropriated and made available to the landless farm workers in several ways.

The industrialization program brought nearly 1,000 new factories to the economy by the end of June, 1964. They have furnished jobs for 54,000 persons directly and about 60,000 indirectly. The products manufactured by the new plants include: clothing, shoes, radios and television sets, electric home appliances, tools and dies, surgical instruments, chemicals and pharmaceuticals, plastics, electronic devices, cement, glass, optical products, and hundreds of others.

These results have been achieved by governmental "technical assistance" to industrialists interested in location and marketing problems, by help in the selection and training of personnel, by temporary tax exemptions (except for "runaway" plants), by building factories for rent at reasonable rates, and by wide-scale and imaginative publicity and promotion.

The spring of 1956 was marked with a celebration when the Puerto Rican economy passed the dividing line between an industrial country and an agricultural country. For the first time income from manufacturing exceeded income from farming. Income originating from agriculture grew from $70,500,000 in 1939-40 to $199,700,000 in 1960-61, or by 183 per cent; but manufacturing income has grown from $26,700,000 to $384,000,000, or 1,338 per cent. By 1963, Puerto Rico had surpassed every Latin American country except oil-rich Venezuela in per capita income. It stood at $740, far above that of three-fourths of the world—but still much less than average income in the United States. The increase from the $121 average in 1939-40 represents a rise of over six times (615 per cent).

Wage-earners' family incomes have increased faster than have family incomes as a whole, as the workers have participated fully in the benefits of industrial development. An even more important indication of worker participation in the benefits of economic advances is what economists call "factor shares" of the national income going into compensation to employees, i.e., in broad terms, the "working class."

Fairly recent analyses (1952-56) of factor shares for 38 of the major countries of the world show Puerto Rico to be third in the world in the proportion received by the workers of hand and brain: United Kingdom, 68.9 per cent; United States, 67.6 per cent; Puerto Rico, 64.4 per cent. Two of the most important Latin American countries show the following experience: Brazil, 41.7 per cent and Peru, 37.8 per cent. Japan's proportion was 47.9 per cent.

Public Health Program

An even more spectacular record has been achieved in the field of health. In 1940 life expectancy at birth was 46 years; today it is over 70 years, equal to that in the United States. In many of the underdeveloped areas of the world, life expectancy is from 35 to 45 years. Malaria has been wiped out; diarrhea and enteritis mortality rates reduced in the period, 1940-61, from 405 deaths per 100,000 population to 36; tuberculosis from 260 to 26; pneumonia from 169 to 38; and nephritis from 108 to 6. The infant mortality rate was cut by more than half; the general death rate was reduced from 18.4 to 6.8 per 1,000 (U.S. rate, 9.3 in 1961).

An extremely sensitive index of the general feeling of well-being of a people is the suicide rate, as Erich Fromm has shown in *The Sane Society*. In 1936 Puerto Rico had the exceedingly high rate of 30.7 per 100,000. By 1946 it had been reduced to 25.4, and by 1960 it was down to 9.7.

An indication of how the public health program reaches even the farm groups may be found in the results of blood tests for syphilis among farm migrant workers in a big Eastern state in 1956:

All Groups (5,375) average positive	12.1 per cent
Ethnic group A (3,500)	15.6 per cent
Ethnic group B (343)	7.6 per cent
Whites, non-Puerto Rican (117)	4.3 per cent
Puerto Ricans (1,115)	2.3 per cent

The high rate of natural increase of population remains a serious threat to further social and economic gains. While the death rate fell by 63.0 per cent between 1940 and 1961, the birth rate fell only 19.5 per cent. Therefore, the rate of natural increase actually rose from 20.1 to 24.2 per 1,000. At this rate, the population will double in 28 years.

Puerto Rico, since 1937, has been committed to a program of allowing free democratic choice of the size of the family to poor people; those well off have never had any problem knowing how to plan the size of their families. The following appear to be the factors responsible for the continuing high birth rate: (1) the farming population still thinks of children as "the social security of the poor" (the rural birth rate is far higher than the city rate); (2) an extremely high percentage of the total population are in the reproductive age categories; and (3) the extent of ignorance about the availability of safe and reliable methods of contraception is wide. Here, as in so many other areas, education is the answer. The 1960 census showed that while the average "ever-married" Puerto Rican woman with no education had produced 6.7 children by the time she was 45, the number of children reflected education in the following direct manner: those with 5-7 years of schooling completed had had 5.1 children; 8 years completed, 3.7; high school diploma, 2.4; 4 years of college, 2.3.

Achievements in Education

Puerto Rico's achievements in the field of both formal and informal education have also been hailed by the thousands of visitors from outside. Illiteracy among the population ten years of age and over has been brought down from 31.5 per cent in 1940 to 12.4 per cent in 1960. Almost all illiterates are found among the older people. Enrollment in public schools rose from 304,000 in 1940 to 635,000 in 1961-62; the number of teachers rose from 6,000 to 15,000; school rooms more than doubled in number; and expenditures for public education rose by 1,038 per cent.

Private schools have increased substantially in numbers and attendance with the rise of a prosperous middle class. They numbered 135 in 1961-62, enrolled 48,488 pupils, and had 1,978 teachers.

Higher education has also expanded phenomenally. The University of Puerto Rico's student body has risen from 4,987 in 1939-40 to 21,262 twenty-two years later. The second oldest university in Puerto Rico, the Inter-American, founded as the Polytechnic Institute in 1912 at San German, now serves some 5,000 students, and the Catholic University, founded in Ponce in 1948, has about the same number. Furthermore, the Puerto Rican Government provides hundreds of scholarships for graduate study in the United States, Spain, Mexico, and other countries.

"Operation Serenity"

Puerto Ricans are living longer; they are consuming more goods; they eat better; their homes are better built and furnished. There is, in Biblical terms, more bread. Muñoz, however, warned his people that "man does not live by bread alone." The past history of industrialization indicates that the pursuit of material gain may outweigh man's pleasure in his family and his friends; may place a dollar sign on relations which formerly had been governed by love, laughter, music, poetry, appreciation of "the good, the true and the beautiful," by comradeship in a common cause, by devotion to one's fellow men. The competition for wealth and status may endanger the Puerto Ricans' deep feeling for the essential dignity and worth of each human being and introduce divisive considerations such as race, religion, color, wealth, or position.

The Commonwealth Constitution speaks of "our fervor for education, our faith in justice, our devotion to the courageous, industrious and peaceful way of life; our fidelity to individual human values above and beyond social position, racial differences, and economic interests; and our hope for a better world based on these principles."

Operation Serenity is a broadly based popular educational program designed to make the people conscious of the rich heritage of Spain in architecture, art, languages, poetry, music, cooking, fiestas, and strong, extended family life, and the need for conserving these habits and customs. Step by step the best of the Anglo-American traditions of democratic institutions, efficient and honest public administration, and advanced technology applied to the production of more wealth are also being incorporated into the Puerto Rican culture.

The crucial role of education in the process of Puerto Rican reconstruction was well stated by Governor Muñoz in his message to the legislature in 1956:

> I earnestly believe that except for the most pressing human wants, education shall constitute our supreme consumption, not only in Puerto Rico and America, but in every part of the world. I speak of education not in the sense of a ration which is merely served to children and youngsters. I mean education which is fed to all throughout a lifetime as an urgent need and a source of joy for the spirit. I refer to that form of education which will endow democracies with a deeper sense of their true significance. This is the only way to conquer poverty and to achieve a state of undisturbed peace throughout the world.

The government's educational television and radio stations help in adult education campaigns, especially in the study of English, and both the adult education program of the Department of Education and the Extension Service of the University of Puerto Rico stress the teaching of English. The other 33 radio and eight television stations also often carry programs in English. It was only after the first elected governor took office in January, 1949, that the ambiguous position of English in the Puerto Rican schools was cleared up. Now English is a required subject from the first grade on.

In addition to regular academic work the public educational system includes the largest vocational school in the world and other features such as universal free lunches, social work, health education, guidance, vocational and physical rehabilitation, and library services, including "bookmobiles" for use in rural areas. The Division of Community Education is of special interest to the rest of the world. It has been one of the major devices for reaching the people with a message of self-help and techniques for helping them help themselves. Its work has been recorded in several prize-winning films, and UNESCO has published a laudatory account of its operation. Despite these advances, much remains to be done in the field of education. As in the United States, teacher loads are too heavy, salaries too low, teacher training inadequate.

Puerto Rico's rapid social and economic development has, indeed, been astonishing. But it is far from complete. Unemployment in 1963-64 averaged 83,000—11 per cent of the labor force. Fortunately, until recently, many Puerto Rican workers had been needed in the United States; a large proportion had been drained off into our labor market here, some on a seasonal basis on the farms, others permanently.

This has had its disadvantages, too, since so many of the migrants have been among the best trained and more ambitious members of the labor force. Puerto Rico has been in the same position as so many European countries in the past: raising manpower at a considerable cost for housing, public services, education, etc., and then losing them at the age of their highest productivity. For decades, the farm population of the States has played the same role for the industrial cities. Both paid the penalty for producing children faster than they could expand their economies.

Years ago, people in Puerto Rico began to solve this problem for themselves. They came to the States on their own. Figure 1 in Chapter 4 shows the ups and downs of the movement. Let us look at it more closely.

THE PUERTO RICAN JOURNEY

Even before 1898 the hope of leading a better life drew Puerto Ricans to the United States. One of the settlers in the early 1890's was Arthur Schomburg who created the Schomburg Collection of the New York Public Library. In 1910, the census found Puerto Ricans living in 39 states, plus Hawaii. By 1920, only four states had no Puerto Ricans. Each succeeding census has recorded persons from Puerto Rico in all states. Even sub-Arctic Alaska had 562 Puerto Ricans in 1960.

Let us follow the process of dispersion. The Puerto Rican communities of Hawaii and California, for example, resulted from the recruiting of sugar cane workers by Hawaiian employers and of cotton field hands by Arizona employers. Some of the recruits en route to Hawaii liked California and stayed there. Still others returned to the West Coast after living in Hawaii. Their numbers were later augmented by those who left Arizona. Succeeding migration occurred, so that from 1910 to 1950 the second largest state of Puerto Rican settlement was California. New Jersey had replaced it by 1960, with Illinois in third place and California in fourth.

The 1929 "crash," the Great Depression and the Second World War almost halted Puerto Rican migration for some time. The end of the wartime transportation restrictions and the labor shortages of the post-war period again brought recruiters to the Island. New

York City, which has the largest labor market in the world, again began to attract Puerto Ricans. Planeloads of workers also left Puerto Rico for many cities outside New York under charter to private, fee-charging labor contractors. These contractors often abused workers and employers alike. Workers were hired to fill jobs for which they were inexperienced and untrained and for which their employers had been promised "skilled help." Both were charged a fee by the contractor, who also made a commission on transportation fares and sometimes sold such necessary items as suitcases, clothing, and other merchandise.

The Labor Department of the Puerto Rican government became alarmed at this unethical traffic in human beings and recommended corrective legislation. In 1947 and 1948, such legislation was adopted by the Puerto Rican legislature. Offices to assist the migrants and the receiving communities were first established in New York and Chicago. Now the Migration Division of the Department of Labor maintains offices in San Juan and eleven mainland cities. The division's personnel now work in 115 mainland towns and cities each year.

Cooperation was also established between the Puerto Rico Employment Service and the United States Employment Service. It was agreed that since Puerto Ricans were United States citizens, they should be included in the domestic labor force. This meant that job orders passing through the regular clearance procedures of the U. S. Employment Service were to be sent to the Puerto Rican Employment service when qualified local workers were not available. A second result of this cooperative arrangement was that employers could not legally recruit labor in Puerto Rico without an official approval from the Puerto Rican government, which in turn was granted only when a legitimate order was cleared through the regular U. S. Employment Service channels.

Broader Puerto Rican Dispersion

Today Puerto Ricans are much more widely dispersed than they have been for over 30 years. Broader settlement has come about as a result of the combined activities of the two governments, the operations of the farm program, and, principally, the widespread labor shortages in many areas of the States. Between 1950 and 1960, the Puerto Rican population outside New York City increased 404 per cent, while that in the city rose only 150 per cent.

The 1960 census shows 892,513 Puerto Ricans living in the 50 states: 617,056 were born in Puerto Rico; 275,457 were born here of Puerto Rican parentage. New York City contained 612,574 (68.6 per cent of the U. S. total), of whom 429,710 had been born in Puerto Rico and 182,864 here. New York City's proportion had dropped from 88 per cent in 1940 to 83 per cent in 1950 and to 69 per cent in 1960.

The 1960 census reported Puerto Rican-born persons living in all but one (Duluth-Superior) of the 101 Standard Metropolitan Statistical Areas of over 250,000 population.

Communities of over 500 persons born in Puerto Rico were reported as follows: Allentown-Bethlehem-Easton, 1,059; Baltimore, 924; Boston, 1,249; Bridgeport, 4,371; Buffalo, 2,052; Chicago, 25,416; Cleveland, 3,124; Detroit, 1,254; El Paso, 665; Ft. Lauderdale-Hollywood, 811; Gary-Hammond-East Chicago, 4,221; Hartford, 2,360; Honolulu, 930 (Hawaii is the only state in which the second-generation outnumbered the first, 3,092 to 1,197); Jersey City, 10,784; Lancaster, Pa., 541; Los Angeles-Long Beach, 7,214; Miami, 8,687; Milwaukee, 2,223; Newark, 8,958; New Haven, 962; New Orleans, 718; Paterson-Clifton-Passaic, 6,641; Philadelphia-Camden, 15,735; Reading, 508; Rochester, 1,493; San Antonio, 757; San Diego, 648; San Francisco-Oakland, 4,068; San Jose, 955; Springfield-Chicopee-Holyoke, 875; Tacoma, 811; Tampa-St. Petersburg, 1,008; Trenton, 1,559; Washington-Md.-Va., 2,427; Wilmington, 586; Youngstown-Warren, 1,820. These numbers would be increased if the locally born were added; e.g., Chicago's total would be 35,361. There are also a number of smaller communities in smaller areas and in non-metropolitan urban areas, e.g., Norfolk, Va., 386, Lorain, Ohio, 2,471; Vineland, N. J., 926; Palm Beach, Fla., 1,377; Meriden, Conn., 710; and Waterbury, Conn., 743.

If there is no serious setback to the American economy, further dispersion will very likely continue, even though New York still requires new workers for its industries, particularly in the needle trades.

Naturally, Puerto Ricans are highly vulnerable to fluctuations in the economy. The economic contraction of 1953-54 hit these migrants with special severity. In just six months one prosperous Ohio Puerto Rican community of around 3,000 shrank to 900.

Most returned to Puerto Rico, where friends and relatives helped them until jobs again became available, just as Southerners in the industrial North traveled south again to their former homes. This is only one of the numerous parallels between the movement of Puerto Ricans and other internal migrants, and even to many of our immigrant ancestors.

As a rule and as a matter of public policy, the Commonwealth of Puerto Rico neither encourages nor discourages migration. The government recognizes that until the island's economic development has reached a point where greater job opportunities and economic security can be offered to its workers than can be found on the mainland, ambitious citizens who are able to do so will search elsewhere. Therefore, the government strives to help those who decide to leave to adjust more quickly to their new home community. On the other hand, whenever increasing numbers of Puerto Ricans lose their jobs in the States, as they do during dips in the business cycle, prospective migrants are urged to make doubly sure they have jobs before going to the mainland.

The Integration Process

The orientation program for persons planning to move to the U. S. attempts to cover the entire island, since freedom of movement belongs to the Puerto Rican as well as to any citizen of the United States. Each week the 33 radio stations throughout the Island carry a program, "Guide to the Traveler," based on the experiences of previous migrants. The entire force of the nine local offices of the Puerto Rican Employment Service aids in the orientation process, using labor market information received through United States Employment Service channels. Local committees on migrant orientation exist in all the towns in Puerto Rico. Television and newspapers are used regularly, and millions of copies of leaflets also help the guidance process. The simply written, attractively illustrated and printed leaflets deal with such subjects as the urgency of knowing English, climate and clothing in the States, the documents which are needed for schools and other institutions, the need for a driver's license when one purchases a car, warnings against the wiles of installment sellers, and a wide variety of other topics.

The Migration Division issues additional material in the States and works with the Puerto Ricans individually and in groups, as well as with the receiving communities, to speed up the adjustment process.

Each year since 1949, the Migration Division has organized a campaign in New York City to urge the newcomer to go to night school to learn or improve his English and vocational skills. Some 200,000 to 300,000 leaflets are issued annually, radio appeals are made in Spanish, and the aid of teachers, priests, preachers, police, and social workers, both Puerto Rican and non-Puerto Rican, is enlisted to help fill the night classes. More recently the campaign has been extended to all of the other major areas where Puerto Ricans live and work.

Specialized literature is produced and distributed as needed. Each election year a campaign is organized urging the Puerto Rican to register and vote. Suggestions are published on how to prepare oneself for and how to seek a better job. Sometimes special classes are organized to help people prepare for specific job openings when a fair number are soon to become available. More often the vocational schools of the local communities are utilized, although they are not always available to the newcomer who is not yet in the industry in which he would like to work.

The Puerto Rican as Our New Neighbor

We have seen that the newcomer comes from a culture in which strong emphasis is placed on education and on cooperative effort to improve conditions. The effort has been crowned with considerable success. Why, then, does he leave? The answer would have to vary with the individual but it is possible to generalize for the big majority. They leave because they want to progress even faster than they can in the Commonwealth; they are benefitting from "Operation Bootstrap"—but not enough to become satisfied. There is an old German saying, "The appetite grows with eating." Once hope and ambition have been aroused, the urge to fulfill them increases. In other words, those who have achieved some success in the Commonwealth desire even more. Overwhelmingly, these are the people who leave. The migrants are more likely to have had industrial experience than members of the labor force in Puerto Rico; more likely to be skilled, and less than half as likely to be unskilled. They are much more likely to have come from cities.

A physical anthropological study in 1948-49 found "that migrants have enjoyed a better socio-economic background which is expressed through more adequate diet and better health, in larger body dimensions."

The migrant stream contains a much larger proportion of persons able to read and write than does the whole population of Puerto Rico. About 50 per cent of the new arrivals speak English but many are timid about trying their new skill before strangers. However, a 1957 survey made by Pulse, Inc., for radio station WHOM, found 63 per cent of the Puerto Rican families in New York City speaking English at home. Many more can read English, and many speak English on the job and in other situations outside the home.

Once here, the newcomer has to adjust to his new home. Many have serious problems, of course, and, again, these problems will vary with the migrant's background. Those from rural areas experience more difficulty in cities than their urban compatriots. Those from the mountainous coffee area tend to be individualistic, while those from the sugar cane plantations are more accustomed to cooperative action, to working in groups. Both Julian Steward and his associates and Theodore Brameld have defined further cultural differences which might affect the migrant's adjustment to the United States.

Now let us look at what our Puerto Rican neighbor is doing to become integrated into his new surroundings. What kind of a job does he have? Where and how does he live? How extensively does he participate in church and community affairs? It is in these areas that the new citizens express the values most important to them. Dr. Elena Padilla, a Puerto Rican anthropologist, writes in her book, *Up From Puerto Rico,* on life in an East Harlem slum section that:

> For recent migrants, the most important and most desirable life goals and adaptations in New York are: working hard and being a "good" worker; valuing formal education and schooling; learning English while not forgetting how to speak Spanish; cultivating the desire to "progress" and get ahead, or "to get the feet off the dish," particularly through the education of one's children; being brave and assertive; not letting anyone take advantage of oneself, or "take you for a ride" (*no dejarse coger de bobo*); being quiet; being careful in the selection of friends and trusting only a few; and preferring the unity

and continuity of relationships with one's own family and cooperating and helping those relatives and close friends who are in need.

How Does He Make His Living?

The Columbia University study found that 85 per cent of the migrants had quit jobs in Puerto Rico to come to the States. What the typical migrant sought was not a job as such; it was a *better* job. It has already been noted that he is better educated and more likely to have had industrial experience than the worker who stays on the island. Generally, the Puerto Rican's first job in the United States will bring him more money, but a lower job classification, than he had in Puerto Rico.

Yet Puerto Rican labor is vital to the economic future of the many areas of the United States. For decades our country has had to call in the extra workers it needs. The Harvard New York Metropolitan Region Study announced that:

> The rate of Puerto Rican migration to New York is one of the factors that determine how long and how successfully the New York metropolitan region will retain industries which are under competitive pressure from other areas.
>
> To the extent that some of these industries have hung on in the area, they have depended on recently arrived Puerto Rican workers, who have entered the job market of the New York area at the rate of about 13,000 each year. But the New York area is beginning to lose its unique position as the first stopping-off place for Puerto Rican immigrants; this stream of migration is now spreading to other mainland areas as well, and the spread promises to accelerate.

New York is the center of the garment industry, the economic mainstay of the city. A recent report concluded that "if it [the needle trades] moved elsewhere en masse, we could expect New York's population to shrink by about 3,000,000 people." This industry is an excellent source of employment for newly arrived Puerto Ricans because, as the same report states, "they are quick to learn and have above-average manual dexterity." A needle-trades worker in Manhattan, where three-fourths of the industry is located, "earns almost 60 per cent more than does the garment worker located elsewhere."

Other industries and services which find the new workers highly satisfactory include: steel foundries and metal fabricators, plastics, hotels and restaurants, food-processing plants, electronics, optical and surgical instruments, jewelry, merchant marine, laundries, hospitals, building maintenance, and welding. New York's 40,000 factories include over 300 industries, and Puerto Ricans are found in almost all of them. Each month 1,500 new corporations are created in New York City. Three hundred of these are engaged in manufacturing. As the City Commerce Department reported in 1959, "What generates these new businesses and keeps the old ones stable or expanding is the city's labor supply. Its greatest resource is manpower."

The Harvard Report indicates that:

> The adjustment patterns of Puerto Rican residents of the region are following roughly the same course as that of earlier waves of immigration from Europe, with due allowance for some cultural differences. Their job opportunities and job skills are improving and their cultural patterns and aspirations are changing in ways which conform more closely to the mainland environment. Negroes in the region, too, are rapidly adopting the values and aspirations typical of a white urban area, but their ability to realize them faces greater obstacles than those confronting the white Puerto Ricans.

As anti-discrimination laws become more effective and public opinion becomes increasingly less biased, the Negro should find his relative disadvantage declining.

The 1960 census found the following distribution of jobs among employed Puerto Rican males in the New York area:

Semi-skilled (operatives)	41.0%
Service	19.2
Clerical and sales	11.5
Craftsmen and foremen	10.5
Professional, managerial, technical, and proprietors	5.4
Unskilled	5.4
Miscellaneous	7.0

Women, of course, are highly concentrated in the operatives category (65.3 per cent); followed by clerical and sales, (15.3 per cent); and then by service trades (7 per cent). However, there were only 514 Puerto Rican domestic servants in the entire area. On the other end of the scale there were 2,721 Puerto Rican women listed in professional, technical, managerial, and related fields.

Unfortunately, census data for comparisons of 1950 and 1960 occupational figures for New York City are not available. We do have data, however, for the United States as a whole for first and second-generation Puerto Ricans. They are given in the following table:

MALES

Occupational grouping	Puerto Rican born	Puerto Rican parentage
Professional, technical, managerial, etc.	5.3%	12.4%
Clerical and sales	9.3	18.4
Craftsmen, foremen, etc.	10.1	16.7
Operatives	40.0	26.4
Service (except domestic)	17.7	10.6
Laborers (except farm and mine)	8.3	7.4
Farm and mine laborers	3.1	1.3
Miscellaneous and not reported	6.2	6.8

It will be noted that the first two groups, which make up the "white collar" occupations, more than doubled as a proportion of those employed between the first and second generations (from 14.6 per cent to 30.8 per cent).

The increase in the white collar occupations was much sharper among the Puerto Rican women than among the men: first generation, 16.4 per cent; second, 57.4 per cent. This is slightly above the average for all employed women in the United States, 54 per cent. There was a drop of about two-thirds in the "operatives" category: from the first generation's 66.3 per cent to 22.6 per cent for the second generation. These data, especially those for the needle trades, will sound familiar to all students of our immigration history.

What incomes do the Puerto Ricans get for their work? Here again, we find increases varying in much the same manner as do those of other workers. Income reported in the 1960 census was

$2,533 for the U.S. as a whole, compared with $1,654 reported in the 1950 census. Those who were farmers reported incomes of $1,434; rural non-farm dwellers received $1,857 and urban dwellers averaged $2,555.

First and second-generation differences between 1950 and 1960 incomes reported are as follows:

	Puerto Rican born	Puerto Rican parentage
1950	$1,664	$1,526
1960	$2,513	$2,868

But there is the factor of age to be taken into account. Earnings increase toward "middle age" and then, except in the case of highly educated professionals, tend to decline. But the average age of the Puerto-Rican-born person in the States is 27.9; that of the second-generation is 5.9. Obviously, if we are to compare first and second generation earnings fairly, we must offset the age factor. This we can do by using the same age group. Let us see what happens when we compare the 25-34 category for the United States as a whole and the four states for which the 1960 census furnishes income data:

	1st generation	2nd generation
United States	$2,687	$3,519
California	$3,183	$3,944
Illinois	$3,208	$4,042
New Jersey	$2,782	$3,677
New York	$2,631	$3,466

Another answer to the question, "Are the Puerto Ricans climbing the economic ladder?" is found in the 1960 census data for median family income for New York City's five counties and three "next door" counties:

New York (Manhattan)	$3,459
Kings (Brooklyn)	$3,868
Bronx	$4,108
Westchester	$4,890

Richmond (Staten Island)	$5,136
Suffolk	$5,594
Queens	$5,756
Nassau	$6,665

Interesting corollary data concern the use of consumer goods by Puerto Ricans in New York City. Eighty per cent of the households have one radio; 79.9, a TV set; 93.3, an electric refrigerator; and 41.9, a telephone. Cars are owned by 19 per cent.

The only industry in New York City in which Puerto Rican employment has been studied in detail is in hotels. A survey of 33 major hotels employing more than 20,000 persons showed that 21 per cent of these are Puerto Rican. Every hotel questioned employed at least some Puerto Ricans. with the proportion ranging from 7 to 28 per cent of the total staff. Usually, the newcomers occupy "behind-the-scenes" jobs, but the report notes that they "have achieved a substantial breakthrough into skilled and supervisory work." It concludes that, "as language barriers are reduced and skills acquired, it is anticipated that their employment in better-paying jobs will be accelerated."

There remains one important established area of making a living in big cities—organized crime. There is no indication that the Puerto Ricans are playing any important role in the rackets. It may be that, like the Negroes, they either have no inclinations toward this type of business career or they are kept out by the closely knit ethnic groups which are already in control. There are indications that nepotism is the general rule among the more successful rackets.

Dan Wakefield, a shrewd political reporter, brings up a point which should worry every civic-minded person. He writes, in his fascinating book, *Island in the City:*

> One of the few distinctions so far between the Puerto Ricans and the early immigrant groups to New York City is that the Puerto Ricans have developed no criminal gangs of adults as the Irish, Jews, and Italians did. This is perhaps a happy fact for the social workers but may in the long run be a sad one for the progress of the Puerto Ricans. Many old-time observers in the city believe this lack of an adult underworld is one of the reasons why Puerto Ricans have not yet achieved any power in politics.

Puerto Ricans and Other Low-income Groups

We have seen that the Puerto Ricans *are* climbing up the economic ladder. However, there are still far too many persons in New York City living in poverty, including the most recent of the newcomers—the Puerto Ricans. The Mayor's Council on Poverty released the following figures in April, 1964: some 1,500,000 persons, or about one in every five New Yorkers, live in poverty. This includes some 1,200,000 persons living in 389,000 families, plus 320,000 persons living alone or with non-relatives. About 214,000 of the families are white, non-Puerto Rican; 106,000 are non-white; and 69,000 are headed by a Puerto Rican. This means that 18 per cent of the "poor" families are Puerto Rican; 27 per cent are non-white and 55 per cent are "others." These proportions should be compared with 7 per cent, 12 per cent, and 81 per cent, respectively, of all families in New York City. This means that the Puerto Ricans are represented among the "poor" families about two and a half times as often as among New York's families as a whole; the non-white, two and a quarter times as often, and the rest only 68 per cent as often.

One in four dwelling units in the city is dilapidated or deteriorating. They are concentrated in 90 of the city's 2,160 census tracts. Overcrowding, lower educational achievement, unemployment at least double the city rate, high infant mortality rates, high relief rates, and high delinquency rates are also concentrated in these areas as are the dwellings of the most recent arrivals. The city's housing and urban renewal programs were reorganized in April, 1964, in an attempt to speed up the construction of low-rent housing units and clear the slums, step by step with a city-wide campaign to alleviate poverty. The most optimistic forecast is that slums may be eliminated in 40 years!

Even within the slum environment, however, there are significant differences in such vital phenomenon as infant mortality rates. Differential rates per 1,000 live births such as the following have existed in New York City for more than a decade:

	1951	1963
White, non-Puerto Rican	21	20
Puerto Rican born	30	28
Non-white	38	39

These rates are a reflection not only of poverty and poor nutrition, but also of prenatal care. The differentials may be due to a considerable extent to the fact that non-white women are at work in far larger proportion than are Puerto Rican women.

Another impressive set of comparisons is provided by the illegitimacy data for Puerto Ricans and non-whites, by neighborhoods. A 1961 study found great variation:

> The percentage of out-of-wedlock births among the non-whites varied from a high of 37.5 per cent in the Central Harlem district, considered one of the worst slum districts in the city, to a comparative low of 8.9 per cent in the Pelham Bay district, generally regarded as a good residential neighborhood. Similarly, a variation was found among the Puerto Ricans, with a high rate of 21.4 per cent in the Riverside district, where housing conditions are extremely bad, to a low of 3 per cent in the Westchester district, where housing conditions are much better. . . . The ethnic distribution of pregnant school girls was 69.5 per cent non-white, 17.0 per cent Puerto Rican and 11.2 per cent white.

INTEGRATION INTO THE LARGER COMMUNITY

An examination of a wide range of the 1950 census data for 19 national, racial, and ethnic groups led the University of Chicago demographer Donald J. Bogue to conclude that the characteristics of the Puerto Rican group "suggest a rapid assimilation." He continues:

> The educational attainment, income, and occupational level of second-generation Puerto Ricans is clearly superior to that of the Negro population as a whole. In fact, although the evidence is skimpy, it suggests that Puerto Ricans may become assimilated as fast as the Italians, the Polish, and the Czechs have, and much faster than the Negroes and Mexicans.

We have seen that an outstanding settlement house worker, Miss Maryal Knox, felt the same way on the basis of her personal experience. Another professional in the field of helping newcomers is the executive director of the New York Mission Society, which has existed for 105 years to help speed up the integration process of strangers arriving in New York City.

The Reverend David W. Barry said in 1957:

> No previous immigrant group so quickly numbered among its members so many policemen and welfare workers, teachers and social workers, office workers and independent businessmen, and even doctors and lawyers—after barely a dozen years in New York. And the signs of the future are in the substantial enrollment of young Puerto Ricans in the city's colleges and universities.

His view is supported by the existence of substantial organizations in the business and professional fields, such as the Puerto Rican Merchants' Association, with its 5,000 members; the 40-year-old Puerto Rican Civil Service Employees Association, with its own building and a successful credit union; the Spanish Club of the New York City Police Department, with 300 members, 90 per cent of whom are Puerto Ricans; the Association of Puerto Rican Social Workers, with more than 100 members; the Puerto Rican Bar Association with 75 members; the medical association with over sixty; the Puerto Rican Teachers' Association, with about 100 of the 250 Puerto Rican teachers, psychologists, counselors, and other personnel of the school system; and organizations of nurses, ministers, electricians, barbers, bar owners, taxi owners and drivers, and baseball umpires.

A Philadelphia report, in the late 1950's, noted the "entrepreneurial superiority" of the Puerto Rican. It listed many Puerto Rican-owned businesses, "but the most typical . . . are the 'bodegas,' or Spanish-style grocery stores." In Philadelphia there was one such store in 1948; by 1956 there were 40; today there are over 80. It is estimated that in mid-1964 there were almost 4,000 bodegas and 2,800 other Puerto Rican-owned stores, barber shops, and restaurants.

The Philadelphia Commission on Human Relations, analyzing the 1960 census data, found two groups of Puerto Ricans: those of recent arrival (Group A) who were concentrated in 12 census tracts near the center of the city, and (Group B) those with longer residences, who were scattered throughout 129 of the remaining census tracts. Group B showed a higher level of education (with 21 per cent having finished high school, contrasted to 4 per cent in Group B), a lower rate of unemployment, a higher median income, fewer women employed, a slightly higher median age, and a lower proportion of persons born in Puerto Rico.

A similar study of New York City would undoubtedly show that the equivalent of Group A would be found concentrated in the 90 census tracts already mentioned as "pockets of poverty," with the others scattered throughout most of the remainder of the 2,160 census tracts plus the suburbs. Puerto Ricans in 1960 lived in 1,598 of all the city's census tracts, i.e., 74 per cent of them.

Outside New York and Philadelphia, Puerto Ricans also work in a variety of fields, steel being the most common. Seasonal work on farms attracts about 25,000 Puerto Ricans annually, most of whom return home in the fall. The majority of the agricultural workers are employed under a work agreement formulated by the Puerto Rico Department of Labor and the United States Employment Service. The agreement provides for: a guaranteed minimum term of employment; the prevailing wage for the area; workmen's compensation insurance even when it is not required by state law; adequate and hygienic housing; the control of payroll deductions when the employer has advanced transportation funds; group sickness and accident policies; inspection of the worker's employment records by field representatives of the Puerto Rico Migration Division; and, finally, freedom from discrimination on the basis of race, color, creed, or labor union membership or activity. An idea of the importance of Puerto Rican farm workers to the economy of New Jersey comes from a report that in 10 years 62,804 of them had aided in the harvesting of produce worth $633,000,000. New Jersey is one of the 12 states in which Puerto Ricans are an important element in farm labor.

Generally, the farm worker is less well off than his more highly skilled compatriot. Those who come "on their own," rather than under the work agreement, are likely to find living and working conditions poor. A report in 1959 on Puerto Rican farm workers in the New Haven area, for example, found that "85 per cent of the farms provide housing which is substandard." Workers were recruited illegally in New York City for many of these farms.

Participation in Civic Affairs

One of the most important goals of "Operation Bootstrap" is the involvement of Puerto Rican citizens in the working out of their own destiny. This, of course, is the essence of democracy. And democracy depends, at a minimum, on the citizen's exercise of his voting rights. In this crucial expression of freedom, Puerto Ricans are far more active than most of the free world. In recent years the vote in Puerto Rico has seldom fallen below 75 per cent of those eligible, and several times it has been at least 80 per cent. Democratic attitudes are also reflected in the fact that there are five women mayors in Puerto Rico, one Commonwealth Senator, three members of the Commonwealth House of Representatives, and 97 elected to municipal assemblies.

There are no studies showing how long it takes Puerto Rican migrants to achieve a higher participation in civic affairs. Studies of other groups, however, report that it takes an English-speaking newcomer up to five years to attain the amount of participation shown by the local citizens. One such study reports that "rural migrants take 10 years or more before they equal the native in proportion registered, whereas urban migrants exceed the natives after only five years." Other studies indicate that voluntary organizations other than labor unions and churches are not effective media for drawing working-class citizens into community activity. Such organizations appeal largely to the white-collar and/or professional middle class.

Unions, however, are undeniably important as civic organizations. They have daily contact with large numbers of voters, whom they frequently urge to register and go to the polls. Puerto Ricans have evidently been responsive to the efforts of unions to interest them in political and community activities. The Columbia University study in 1948 showed that 51 per cent of the Puerto Ricans in the labor force belonged to unions. There is every reason to believe that this percentage has risen—a 1959 Pulse survey showed 63 per cent of New York's Spanish-language households contained one or more union members.

Puerto Rican civic organizations have helped enormously in "getting out the vote." The Council of Puerto Rican and Spanish-American Organizations of Greater New York, which was founded in 1952 and now consists of dozens of civic, social, cultural, religious, and fraternal organizations, in each recent election year has set up stations at which persons are advised on various aspects of their civic duty, including taking the literacy test. The campaign is non-partisan and follows the techniques worked out by the League of Women Voters. The Federation of Puerto Rican Organizations of New Jersey, with 30 member groups, and similar organizations in every Puerto Rican community on the mainland, carry out such campaigns. The Puerto Rican vote in New York City rose from about 35,000 in the 1954 election to about 85,000 in 1956. As the result of intensive registration campaigns carried out through the combined efforts of the Commonwealth of Puerto Rico's Migration Division, Puerto Rican community groups, the Spanish-language press, radio, and theaters, and the political parties, total Puerto Rican and Hispanic registration in New York City rose to about 175,000 (*New York Times,* November 23, 1963)—a remarkable achievement for a group the majority of whose members has been in New York for less than two decades.

All three political parties in New York City (Democratic, Republican, and Liberal) place great emphasis on work among the Puerto Ricans. Puerto Rican ranks now include three state legislators, two city magistrates, and a number of appointive officials in the executive branch of the city and state governments. The first Puerto Rican elected to the New York State Assembly, in 1937, was a Republican. The next, a Democrat, was elected in 1953 and re-elected in 1954, 1956, and 1958, but resigned in 1959 to become a city court judge. He was joined in 1958, 1960, and 1964 by other Democrats.

In addition, there is a Puerto Rican commissioner of the State Human Rights Commission, a city commissioner of urban relocation, the city tax collector, deputy commissioners of corrections and of real estate, and a member of the Board of Higher Education. There are Puerto Rican members on 17 of the 25 local school boards in the city, and five district party leaders, three Democrats and two Republicans.

Outside New York City, the Puerto Rican newcomer has sometimes innocently become involved in political conflicts when he has tried to do his democratic duty. One big city's dominant party is split into two factions. The Puerto Ricans, following their pattern in the Commonwealth, began to register to vote as soon as their year's residence was completed. But they registered in the ranks of the "wrong" faction for their neighborhood. Bricks through the windows carried notes explaining their mistake! A similar event in another big city revolved around voting for the "wrong" candidate. The losing candidate organized reprisals which completely wrecked two Puerto Rican homes. Civic education takes a variety of forms!

THE HOUSING STORY

There is much more to community participation than voting. Housing is perhaps the most important area from the standpoint of the family. Here the Council of Spanish-American Organizations has made a great contribution. Together with the New York City office of the Migration Division, it has established "housing clinics" which provide free weekly counseling service to Puerto Ricans in many New York City neighborhoods. A manual based on the experience of these housing clinics, which are staffed entirely by volunteers, has been written up and distributed to groups wanting to establish similar clinics in other localities. Several cities have already done so. These clinics cannot solve the nationwide shortage of adequate housing for low-income groups; they can, however, lead to substantial improvement in existing housing insofar as tenants, janitors, and landlords have it in their power to improve existing deleterious practices.

In addition, a group called Solidaridad Puertorriqueño has now been formed to rehabilitate many so-called "hopeless" buildings. Its first building, in Brooklyn, has been an outstanding success. Mutual aid home-building has been undertaken in Lorain, Ohio, and East Chicago, Indiana, with good results.

Two other organizations have recently joined the Council in its activity on urban renewal in New York City. These are the Federation of Hispanic Societies, a group representing middle-class settled Spanish-speaking residents, and the Puerto Rican-Hispanic Leadership Forum. Its membership is made up of lawyers, doctors, dentists, social workers, and teachers. The council and the federation presented testimony on housing before the Federal Commission on Civil Rights, and both have been active in campaigns concerning legislative proposals both in New York City and in Albany.

Many New York Puerto Ricans are already homeowners. They live in areas which extend from the eastern tip of Long Island across to the west shore of the Hudson and up into Westchester County. That the same thing is happening in other areas is indicated by a story from the Cleveland *Press* (May 12, 1959). The statement is that of Louis M. Cowan, an experienced realtor:

> A lot of Puerto Ricans plan to settle permanently and buy homes in the area. . . . We've found them to be good financial risks, making

their payments on time. They are becoming a credit to the community, although many of the old-timers protested when they moved in.

On May 3, 1959, the real estate section of *The New York Times* carried a similar story, indicating that "several thousand homes have been sold to Puerto Ricans in the last few years" in New York City. The 1960 census showed 7,396 homes owned by Puerto Ricans in New York City; 18 per cent of those in Philadelphia owned their own homes.

Puerto Ricans also have a good record in public housing. A few years ago, the secretary of the New York Housing Authority reported on the reactions of managers of public housing projects to Puerto Rican tenants. The managers said that "the housekeeping habits of the Puerto Rican tenants were above average," the promptness of rent payments about average, and vandalism on the part of children distinctly less than among other groups. In June, 1962, Puerto Ricans occupied 17.3 per cent of New York City's public housing units; Negroes, 39.6 per cent; whites, 43.1 per cent; and Asians, 0.3 per cent.

Community Development

The Council of Spanish-American Organizations also works with parent associations, community centers and similar groups. Here is an example of how rewarding such civic action can be. The parents association of a school in East Harlem, a school which is about 92 per cent Puerto Rican, was told that the playground would be closed for the summer. There were no funds to pay supervisors. That summer the children played in the streets. Before the following summer, however, a delegation of parents, organized as the Civic Orientation Center, found out how much it would cost to maintain the school's playground facilities. This amount was collected, in nickels, dimes, and quarters, and the kids were brought in off the streets. The results in one index of delinquency alone were spectacular. First summer, 238 broken windows in the school building. Second summer, 23—a reduction of 90 per cent.

This is only one illustration of successful Puerto Rican civic activity. There are many more. The Boy Scouts report that although their East Harlem district is the poorest in the city, it is generally the first to fill its quota in annual finance drives. East Harlem not only fills its quota first, but gives the highest *per capita* average in Manhattan.

One of the fastest-growing activities is represented by the Federation of Hispanic Baseball Leagues. It consists of 31 leagues and includes 190 teams; maintains a commissioner, as the major leagues do; and has a mutual insurance fund for injured players. It organizes many contests between New York City teams and those from Puerto Rican communities throughout Connecticut, New Jersey, and upstate New York.

Recent years have seen the growth of "hometown" associations; by 1961 all 77 *municipios* were represented by organized groups. One of the initial major activities of their federation was the organization of an annual parade. Otherwise, their functions range from purely social to educational and community welfare. Almost all the approximately 300 Puerto Rican organizations in the city now participate in the annual parade.

A National Association for Puerto Rican Civil Rights was in the process of formation in the spring of 1964, influenced by the example of the National Association for the Advancement of Colored People. One of its leaders joined a militant faction of the Negro civil rights groups in calling for a boycott of the New York City schools, but generally the Puerto Rican community seems to prefer a different type of tactic. The local daily newspaper *El Diario-La Prensa,* writing of the Negro battle for desegregation, said: "We are heartily in sympathy with this ideal but we have always believed that the battle of Puerto Ricans is one thing and the battle of the colored people another." No other event in years has caused so much anxiety in the Puerto Rican community. It places far less stress on physical segregation, since most do not suffer from it, and far more on quality education.

And all of their organizations, from the 18-year-old, middle class, literary Instituto de Puerto Rico, through the Puerto Rican Parents' Association, to the United Organizations of the Bronx and the Council of Puerto Rican Organizations of the Lower East Side, are dedicated to the preservation of the best in their Spanish cultural heritage and the absorption of the best of the culture of their new home.

Educational Efforts

One of the earliest efforts of the Puerto Ricans in New York and in many other areas is the creation of organizations to encourage compatriots to pursue their education through college or university. The Puerto Rican Scholarship Fund, the Puerto Rican Association for the Encouragement of Higher Education, the Hispanic Young Adult Association, and the Puerto Rican Youth Bureau were all formed in the late 1940's and early 1950's. In 1961, many of the ablest and most civic minded of the second-generation professionals, working through their Puerto Rican Forum and the Puerto Rican Association for Community Affairs, formed an action agency called ASPIRA. It stated its major problem in the following terms: "The intellectual potential and the creative capacity of the Puerto Rican community are not being developed. Too many Puerto Rican youngsters drop out of high school prior to graduation or discontinue their education upon graduation. Many of those who discontinue their education are unaware of the existence of scholarships, loans, tuition-free schools, and other methods of obtaining a college education."

The goals of ASPIRA are:

—Motivation and orientation of capable Puerto Ricans who are in high school to enter the professional and technical fields.

—The acquisition by Puerto Rican youth of an adequate self-image through the study of their cultural heritage, traditions, and leaders.

—The training of Puerto Rican youths with leadership potential so that once they become established in the community they can offer their positions, their skills, and their dedication to the solution of community problems.

ASPIRA's professional staff conducts orientation workshops where students are helped to work out realistic plans for continuing their education. The workshop program includes lectures, information on a wide range of job openings, individual counseling, and working with parents. There is a federation of ASPIRA clubs in the high schools (there were 16 in the spring of 1964). ASPIRA conducts an annual institute on education and community affairs. Some 600 students, in addition to the membership of the high school clubs, were served during the first year.

It has been seen that the school system is making extraordinary efforts to speed up the integration process of the Puerto Rican pupils. But the same problems which plagued most of our immigrant ancestors must be confronted and solved by the Puerto Ricans. A large family which suffers from a small income is tempted to push children toward early entrance into the labor market. This, of course, means drop-outs and "blind alley" jobs.

There are many data indicating that the push toward a higher education is producing results. For example, in the New York area, the percentages of the first- and second-generation Puerto Ricans, 5-24 years of age, attending school in 1960 were:

	1st generation	2nd generation
Male	32.7%	71.4%
Female	30.2	68.4

Since these figures may be highly influenced by age distribution, let us look at the percentages of those of post-high school age, 18-24, attending school in 1960:

Age	Sex	1st generation	2nd generation
18-19	male	18.5%	32.8%
	female	18.2	25.8
20-21	male	6.6	17.6
	female	4.6	10.0
22-24	male	5.0	11.2
	female	2.9	4.7

Next, let us look at the choice of type of high school, academic or vocational, which was made by the three major student groups in 1963 and compare that with the situation in 1957:

	Academic		Per Cent Increase	Vocational	
	1957	1963		1957	1963
Puerto Ricans	50.6%	62.5%	23.3%	49.4%	37.5%
Negroes	64.1	74.0	15.0	35.9	26.0
Others	87.5	88.4	1.0	12.5	11.6

If higher aspirations are indicated by choice of academic over vocational high schools, then 23.3 per cent more Puerto Ricans achieved them between 1957 and 1963 in comparison with 15.0 per cent of the Negroes and less than 1 per cent of the others. It should be understood that it is not necessary to go to college to lead a happy and successful life! But the voracious appetite of cybernetics for white-collar jobs indicates that college, which once was looked upon as a luxury, is rapidly becoming a necessity. Virtually the entire Puerto Rican community is organized to convince their children of this fact.

Religious Activities

Let us look now at the role of religion in the lives of our Puerto Rican newcomers. It is as important in their integration process as in that of most of our ancestors.

Until the Spanish-American War, Puerto Rico was legally Catholic; U. S. Protestant denominations established churches in 1899. They "zoned" the island, assigning a section to each of eight major denominations; created a common theological seminary; and attempted to gain converts. Protestantism is not, then, strange to these newcomers. While 80 to 85 per cent of them are Catholic, the intensity of belief varies widely among geographic regions and social classes. But what about the religious feelings of Puerto Ricans in the United States? The Columbia University study found 83 per cent to be Catholics, 9 per cent Protestants of the long-established denominations, 5 per cent belonging to the "store-front" or less well-known sects, and 2 per cent "spiritualist." A definite variance in intensity of belief between these categories was reflected by figures on the regularity of church attendance. A 1959 survey of Puerto Ricans in the New Haven area showed that while 93 per cent reported church membership, only 26 per cent attended regularly. Findings in New York City showed 25 per cent of the Catholics were regular in attendance, as compared with 50 per cent of the Protestants.

Both Protestant and Catholic churches in all major centers of Puerto Rican settlements provide services not directly related to religion. Elena Padilla reports that relations between Protestant ministers and their Puerto Rican congregations are closer and more personal than between Catholic priests and their parishioners. This may be partly due to the fact that in the 300 Catholic parishes in New York City with Spanish-speaking priests, only two are Puerto Rican, while almost all of the 270-some Protestant churches with Spanish services have Puerto Rican ministers.

According to the Reverend David W. Barry of the City Mission Society, the Puerto Ricans "can't be matched by any previous ethnic group coming to New York City," in terms of money contributed and in hours per week devoted to church work. The per capita contribution of members of churches affiliated with the society is $65 a year, with some of the churches averaging more than $100 per year.

Probably the most comprehensive program among Protestant Puerto Rican churches in New York City is that conducted by the City Mission Society's Church of the Good Neighbor in East Harlem. In one month between 5,500 and 7,500 persons (mostly children and young people) participate in activities sponsored by this church. It sends more than 600 children to camp each summer and conducts the only psychiatric clinic in the city staffed by Spanish-speaking psychiatrists and other professional personnel. To manage this extensive program, the Church of the Good Neighbor maintains a staff of 16 full-time and an equal number of part-time workers.

The Catholic Church has been assisting Puerto Ricans through its settlement house, Casita María, and the substantial work of Catholic Charities and other civic activities carried on by church-related organizations. In 1953, Catholic Spanish Action was created. This organization has cooperated with the Catholic University in Ponce to prepare priests and nuns for work among Spanish-speaking people, has published various kinds of material in Spanish, and has built the annual celebration of San Juan's day in New York City into an imposing affair attended by 35,000 to 40,000 persons. One Puerto Rican commentator observed that many Puerto Rican Protestant families were among those enjoying the floats and pageants of this Catholic celebration. "Why shouldn't they?" he asked. "This is part of the cultural heritage of all Puerto Ricans!"

Perhaps the greatest need of the world today is a willingness on the part of individuals and groups to accept other people on their own terms and not to hold and express the xenophobic attitude,

"Thank God I am not as he," when a member of a different nationality, race, ethnic group, or class passes by. There is among the Puerto Ricans none of the bitter hatred toward other religious groups which so marred the record of our democracy in the days of the Ku Klux Klan, the Know-Nothings, and sporadically, ever since.

It is in the field of race relations especially that the Puerto Rican may make a contribution—if we allow him. Puerto Ricans of dark, light, and white skins have lived together for several centuries without serious discrimination or recrimination, and this healthy attitude can be a model for us. One of the orientation leaflets issued by the Commonwealth is entitled, in Spanish, the equivalent of "When in Rome, Do As the Romans Do." It reminds the migrant that habits and customs differ and that one should watch his neighbor or shopmate for clues to proper actions. It ends by telling the reader, however, that there is one outstanding Puerto Rican virtue: "We don't discriminate against anybody because of his race or the color of his skin. . . . We must continue practicing this wherever we live."

Next, commentators who know the Puerto Rican well stress the contribution he makes with his strong family life, the kind of solidarity which is so often missing from the city scene today.

Others are impressed by his warmth, vitality, friendliness and hospitality, the great value placed on the non-material side of life, on artistic expression, on love of music and dancing, on such indications of cultural values as the fact that the first elected governor of Puerto Rico is widely known as "El Vate," "the Bard." He once wrote poetry and is still proud of it and yearns for the time he might do it again. A former Secretary of Labor (1947-1961) was a playwright—and does not conceal it, as he might if he were a prominent public official in the United States!

Most highly prized of all, and basic to many of the contributions mentioned, is a deep sense of the dignity and worth of the individual.

This crucial element in a meaningful democracy is being introduced into many of our own institutions by the Puerto Rican newcomers; into labor-management relations, for example. Many a foul-mouthed "straw boss," both on farms and in industry, has learned that the brusque, vulgar command is not acceptable to his new employees. He has had to learn the hard way what he should have known already—that self-esteem is an essential ingredient in democratic human relations.

All of these—plus the basic addition to the manpower we need here and the far-reaching assistance Puerto Rico is giving us in our international economic and political relations—are among the contributions of the Puerto Ricans.

Bibliography

ASPIRA: An Agency of the Puerto Rican Forum, Inc., New York, 296 Fifth Avenue, 1963.

Francisco Ayala, "The Transformation of the Spanish Culture," *Puerto Rico: A Study in Democratic Development. The Annals,* V. 285, January, 1953, pp. 104-109.

María Teresa Babín, *The Culture of Puerto Rico.* New York: Migration Division, Department of Labor of Puerto Rico, 1960.

Kurt W. Back, *Slums, Projects and People: Social Psychological Problems of Relocation in Puerto Rico.* Durham, North Carolina: Duke University Press, 1962.

William C. Baggs, "Puerto Rico: Showcase of Development," *1962 Britannica Book of the Year.*

David W. Barry, "Opportunity for Protestant Churches Among Puerto Ricans," *National Council Outlook,* May, 1959.

David W. Barry, "The Puerto Rican Adapts Remarkably," *Washington Post and Times Herald,* May 8, 1959.

Daniel Bell, "Crime as an American Way of Life," *Antioch Review,* Summer, 1953, pp. 131-154.

Elaine Berkowitz, "Family Attitudes and Practices of Puerto Rican and Non-Puerto Rican Pupils," *High Points* (New York), XLIII, No. 3, March, 1961, pp. 25-34.

Max Birnbaum, "Whose Values Should Be Taught?" *Saturday Review,* June 20, 1964, pp. 60-62, 67.

Board of Education, City of New York, *The First Fifty Years: A Brief Review of Progress, 1898-1948.* Fiftieth Annual Report, the Superintendent of Schools, 1949.

Donald J. Bogue, *The Population of the United States.* New York: The Free Press of Glencoe, 1959, pp. 366-374.

David Boroff, "Jews and Puerto Ricans," *Congress Weekly*, April 15, 1957.

Theodore Brameld, *The Remaking of a Culture: Life and Education in Puerto Rico*. New York: Harper, 1959.

Harry C. Bredemeier and Toby Jackson, *Social Problems in America: Costs and Casualties in an Acquisitive Society*. New York: John Wiley, 1963.

William Brink and Louis Harris, *The Negro Revolution in America*. New York: Simon & Schuster, 1964. Based on the *Newsweek* survey, carried in part in July and October, 1963, issues.

Douglass Cater, "Puerto Rico: The Best Answer to Castro," *Reporter*, January 19, 1961, pp. 32-37.

Stuart Chase, *The Proper Study of Mankind*. New York: Harper, 1948.

Henry Chaunicey and John E. Dobbin, *Testing: Its Place in Education Today*. New York: Harper and Row, 1963.

Margaret Clark, *Health in the Mexican-American Culture*. Berkeley and Los Angeles: University of California Press, 1959.

Francisco Collazo, *The Education of Puerto Rican Children in the Schools of New York City*. San Juan: Department of Education Press, 1954.

Petroamérica Pagán de Colón, *Migration Trends*. New York: Migration Division, Department of Labor, Commonwealth of Puerto Rico, 1959.

Petroamérica Pagán de Colón, *The Migrant and the Affluent Society*. New York: Migration Division, Department of Labor of Puerto Rico, 1962.

Commission on Human Relations, City of Philadelphia, *Philadelphia's Puerto Rican Population, with 1960 Census Data*. 1964.

Commission on Human Rights, City of New York. *A Progress Report on Human Rights in New York City, 1955-1962*. New York: The Commission, 1962.

Community Education in Puerto Rico. San Juan: Department of Education, Division of Community Education.

W. Henry Cooke, *Peoples of the Southwest: Patterns of Freedom and Prejudice*. New York: ADL, 1951.

Leonard Covello, *The Heart Is the Teacher*. New York: McGraw-Hill, 1958.

Antonio Cuevas-Viret, "Achievements of the Commonwealth of Puerto Rico in Public Personnel Administration," *Good Government*, October, 1962, pp. 41-43.

S. L. Descartes, *The Economic and Social Situation of Puerto Rico*, 1963. New York: Migration Division, Department of Labor, Commonwealth of Puerto Rico, 1963.

Eileen Díaz, "A Puerto Rican in New York," *Dissent*, VIII, No. 3, Summer, 1961, pp. 383-385.

Manuel Díaz and Roland Cintrón, *School Integration and Quality Education.* New York: Puerto Rican Forum, 1964.

Ernest Dichter, *Pilot Study on How to Implement the Fair Housing Practices Law in New York City.* Croton-on-Hudson, N.Y.: Institute for Motivational Research, Inc., June, 1959. (Study conducted for the New York City Commission on Intergroup Relations.)

"Direct Action in the South," *New South,* V. 18, No. 10-11, October-November, 1963, pp. 1-32.

Daniel Donchian, *A Survey of New Haven's Newcomers: The Puerto Ricans.* New Haven, Conn.: Human Relations Council of Greater New Haven, 1959.

Mary Louise Edwards, *Love Me, Puerto Rico.* Hato Rey: Barton House, 1962.

Stanley Elkins, *Slavery: A Problem in American Institutional and Intellectual Life.* Chicago: University of Chicago Press, 1959.

Charlotte Erickson, *American Industry and the European Immigrant: 1860-1885.* Cambridge: Harvard University Press, 1957.

Robert Ernst, *Immigrant Life in New York City, 1825-1863.* New York: King's Crown Press, 1949.

Harold E. Fey and D'Arcy McNickle, *Indians and Other Americans: Two Ways of Life Meet.* New York: Harper, 1959.

First Report of Continuations Committee, Third Migration Conference, San Juan, Puerto Rico, January 19-26, 1958. New York: City Hall, 1959.

Joseph P. Fitzpatrick, *Delinquency and the Puerto Ricans.* New York: Migration Division, Department of Labor, Commonwealth of Puerto Rico, 1959.

Harry Fleischman, *Let's Be Human.* New York: Oceana Publications, 1960.

Robert F. Foerster, *The Italian Immigration of Our Times.* Cambridge: Harvard University Press, 1924.

Lawrence K. Frank, *Society as the Patient.* New Brunswick: Rutgers University Press, 1948.

John Hope Franklin, *From Slavery to Freedom: A History of American Negroes.* New York: Alfred A. Knopf, 1956.

Frank Freidel, *The Splendid Little War.* Boston: Little, Brown & Co., 1958.

"Full Employment Means Full Mobility," *Life,* March 1, 1954.

John Kenneth Galbraith, *The Affluent Society.* Boston: Houghton Mifflin Co., 1958.

Vincent Gegan and Samuel Thompson, "Worker Mobility in a Labor Surplus Area," *Monthly Labor Review,* Vol. 80, No. 12, December, 1957, pp. 1451-1456.

Harry Golden, "A Short Story of America" in *Only in America.* Cleveland and New York: World Publishing Co., 1958, pp. 127-129.

Lois Gray, *The Puerto Rican Workers in New York.* Paris: Organization for Economic Cooperation and Development, 1963.

Peter Gregory, "The Labor Market in Puerto Rico," in *Labor Commitment and Social Change in Developing Areas.* New York: Social Science Research Council, 1960, pp. 136-172.

Eunice Grier and George Grier, *Privately Developed Interracial Housing: An Analysis of Experience.* (Special Research Report to the Commission on Race and Housing.) Berkeley and Los Angeles: University of California Press, 1960.

Ruth Gruber, *Puerto Rico: Island of Promise.* New York: Hill & Wang, 1960.

Guide to Changing Neighborhoods. New York: National Community Relations Advisory Council, 1956.

Ralph Hancock, *Puerto Rico: A Success Story.* New York: Van Nostrand, 1960.

Oscar Handlin, *The Newcomers.* Cambridge: Harvard University Press, 1959.

Oscar Handlin, *Race and Nationality in American Life.* Garden City, N.Y.: Doubleday Anchor Books, 1957.

Oscar Handlin, *The Uprooted.* Boston: Little, Brown, & Co., 1951.

Earl Parker Hanson, *Puerto Rico: The Land of Wonders.* New York: Alfred A. Knopf, 1960.

Earl Parker Hanson, *Transformation: The Story of Modern Puerto Rico.* New York: Simon & Schuster, 1955.

Michael Harrington, *The Other America: Poverty in the United States.* New York: Macmillan, 1963.

Edward George Hartmann, *The Movement to Americanize the Immigrant.* New York: Columbia University Press, 1948.

Roy B. Helfgott, *Puerto Rican Integration in the Skirt Industry in New York City.* New York: New York State Interdepartmental Committee on Low Incomes and State Commission Against Discrimination, November, 1957.

Vivian W. Henderson, *The Economic Status of Negroes: In the Nation and in the South.* Atlanta: Southern Regional Council, 1963.

Reuben Hill, J. M. Stycos, and Kurt W. Back, *The Family and Population Control: A Puerto Rican Experiment in Social Change.* Chapel Hill: University of North Carolina Press, 1959.

Richard Hofstadter, *Social Darwinism in American Thought, 1860-1915.* Philadelphia: University of Pennsylvania Press, 1944.

A. B. Hollingshead and L. H. Rogler, "Attitudes Toward Slums and Public Housing in Puerto Rico," in *The Urban Condition.* New York: Basic Books, 1963, pp. 229-245.

Edgar M. Hoover and Raymond Vernon, *Anatomy of a Metropolis.* Cambridge: Harvard University Press, 1959.

Karen Horney, *The Neurotic Personality of Our Times.* New York: Norton, 1937.

Langston Hughes and Milton Meltzer, *A Pictorial History of the Negro in America.* New York: Crown, 1956.

Herbert Hyman and Paul B. Sheatsley, "Attitudes Toward Desegregation," *Scientific American,* Vol. 211, No. 1, July, 1964, pp. 16-23.

Noah Jacobs, *Naming-Day in Eden.* New York: Macmillan, 1958.

A. J. Jaffe, *People, Jobs and Economic Development.* Glencoe, Ill.: Free Press, 1959.

A. J. Jaffe, ed., *Puerto Rican Population of New York City.* New York: Bureau of Applied Social Research, Columbia University, 1954.

A. J. Jaffe, *A Survey of Underemployment in Puerto Rico.* New York: Columbia University, Bureau of Applied Social Research, Reprint No. 343, 1961.

Harry Jerome, *Migration and Business Cycles.* New York: National Bureau of Economic Research, 1926.

Arno Jewett, *et al.,* eds., *Improving English Skills of Culturally Different Youth in Large Cities.* Washington: Office of Education, H.E.W., 1964.

Joseph M. Jones, *Does Overpopulation Mean Poverty?* Washington: Center for International Economic Growth, 1962.

Blanche R. Kasindorf, "The Puerto Rican Summer Human Relations Workshop: An Evaluation," *Strengthening Democracy,* January, 1964, pp. 3, 6.

John F. Kennedy, *A Nation of Immigrants.* New York: Harper and Row, 1964. (A revision of the ADL pamphlet.)

William H. Kilpatrick, *Modern Education and Better Human Relations.* New York: ADL, 1949.

Martin Luther King, Jr., *Letter from Birmingham Jail.* Philadelphia: American Friends Service Committee, 1963.

Robert J. Kleiner and Seymour Parker, "Migration and Mental Illness: A New Look," *American Sociological Review,* Vol. 24, No. 5, October, 1959.

Gordon J. Klopf and Israel A. Laster, eds., *Integrating the Urban School.* Proceedings of the Conference on Integration in the New York City Public Schools. New York: Bureau of Publications, Teachers College, Columbia University, 1963.

Simon Kuznets, "Distribution of National Income by Factor Shares," *Economic Development and Cultural Change,* Vol. VII, No. 3, April, 1959, Appendix Table 6.

Simon Kuznets, "Long Swings in the Growth of Population and in Related Economic Variables," *Proceedings of the American Philosophical Society,* Vol. 102, No. 1, February 17, 1958, pp. 25-52.

David Landy, *Tropical Childhood.* Chapel Hill: University of North Carolina Press, 1959.

Thomas S. Langner and Stanley T. Michael, *Life Stress and Mental Health,* Vol. II, The Midtown Manhattan Study. New York: The Free Press of Glencoe, 1963.

Luigi M. Laurenti, *Property Values and Race: Studies in Seven Cities.* (Special Research Report to the Commission on Race and Housing.) Berkeley and Los Angeles: University of California Press, 1960.

Everett S. Lee, *et al., Population Redistribution and Economic Growth, United States, 1870-1950.* Philadelphia: American Philosophical Society, 1957.

Andrew W. Lind, *Hawaii's People.* Honolulu: University of Hawaii Press, 1955.

Samuel Lubell, *The Future of American Politics.* Garden City, N. Y.: Doubleday Anchor Books, 1956.

Benjamin Malzberg and Everett S. Lee, *Migration and Mental Disease.* New York: Social Science Research Council, 1956.

Thomas Mathews, *Puerto Rican Politics and the New Deal.* Gainesville: University of Florida Press, 1960.

Virginia C. Matters, *Meet Puerto Rico.* San Juan: Department of Education on Human Relations, City of Philadelphia, 1959.

Claude McKay, *Harlem: The Negro Metropolis.* New York: Dutton, 1940.

"Meeting the Needs of Puerto Rican Pupils in New York City Public Schools," Special Supplement to *Staff Bulletin,* The Public Schools of New York City, March 28, 1964.

Raymond Metauten, *Puerto Ricans in Philadelphia.* Philadelphia: Commission on Human Relations, City of Philadelphia, 1959.

"Metropolis in Ferment," *Annals of the American Academy of Political and Social Science,* Vol. 314, November, 1957, pp. 1-164.

Mid-Century Pioneers and Protestants. New York: Protestant Council of the City of New York, Department of Church Planning and Research, 1954 (2nd edition).

Herman P. Miller, "Is the Income Gap Closed? 'No!' " *The New York Times Magazine,* November 11, 1962, pp. 50ff.

Herman P. Miller, *Rich Man, Poor Man: The Distribution of Income in America.* New York: Thomas Y. Crowell, 1964.

Walter Millis, *The Martial Spirit.* Boston: Houghton Mifflin Co., 1931.

C. Wright Mills, Clarence Senior, and Rose Kohn Goldsen, *The Puerto Rican Journey: New York's Newest Migrants.* New York: Harper, 1950.

Sidney W. Mintz, *Worker in the Cane: A Puerto Rican Life History.* New Haven: Yale University Press, 1960.

Joseph Monserrat, *School Integration: A Puerto Rican View.* New York: Migration Division, Department of Labor, Commonwealth of Puerto Rico, 1963.

Ashley Montagu, *Education and Human Relations.* New York: Grove-Evergreen, 1958.

Bernice Milburn Moore, *Juvenile Delinquency: Research Theory and Comment.* Washington: National Education Association, Association for Supervision and Curriculum Development, 1958.

James N. Morgan, *et al., Income and Welfare in the United States.* New York: McGraw-Hill, 1962.

J. Cayce Morrison, *The Puerto Rican Study, 1953-1957: A Report on the Education and Adjustment of Puerto Rican Pupils in the Public Schools of the City of New York.* New York: New York City Board of Education, 1958.

Luis Muñoz Marín, *Breakthrough from Nationalism.* (Godkin Lectures given at Harvard University.) New York: Migration Division, Department of Labor of Puerto Rico, 1959.

Gunnar Myrdal, *An American Dilemma: The Negro Problem and Modern Democracy.* New York: Harper and Row, 1962 ed. A condensation of this work is available as Arnold Rose, *The Negro in America.* Boston: Beacon Press, 1956.

The Myths of Racial Integration. New York: American Jewish Congress, 1957.

M. W. Newman, Harry Swegle, and Jack Willner, *The Panic Peddlers.* Chicago: *Chicago Daily News,* 1959. (Reprint of articles published October 13-22, 1959.)

New York Public Schools, 1963-1964. Facts and Figures. Brooklyn: Board of Education, City of New York, 1964.

New York Puerto Rican Radio Audience. New York: Pulse, Inc., October 21-25, 1957. (Survey made for radio station WHOM.)

Albert Jay Nock, quoted in Marie Syrkin, "How Not to Solve 'The Jewish Problem,'" *Common Ground,* Autumn, 1941, pp. 73-78.

Our Changing Community. New York: Community Council of Greater New York, 1957.

Our Puerto Rican Fellow Citizens. Report of a National Conference. New York: AFL-CIO Community Services Committee, 1960.

Elena Padilla, *Up From Puerto Rico.* New York: Columbia University Press, 1958.

Homer Page, *Puerto Rico: The Quiet Revolution.* New York: Viking Press, 1963.

Jean Pakter, Henry Rosner, Harold Jacobziner, and Frieda Greenstein, "Out-of-Wedlock Births in New York City," *American Journal of Public Health,* Vol. 51, No. 5, May, 1961, pp. 683-696, and Vol. 61, No. 6, June, 1961, pp. 846-865.

E. George Payne, "Education and Cultural Pluralism," in *Our Racial and National Minorities.* New York: Prentice-Hall, 1937.

James Peck, *Cracking the Color Line.* New York: Congress of Race Equality, 1959.

The People Take the Lead: A Record of Progress in Civil Rights, 1948-1957. New York: National Labor Service, 1957.

Harvey S. Perloff, *Puerto Rico's Economic Future.* Chicago: University of Chicago Press, 1950.

William Petersen, "Internal Migration and Economic Development in Northern America," *Annals of the America Academy of Political and Social Science,* Vol. 316, March, 1958, pp. 52-59.

Willettee C. Pierce, *Potential Impact of Puerto Rican Americans Eased by Community Planning.* New York: American Federation of International Institutes, 1957. (One of four papers on "The Contribution of Social Work to the Integration of Newcomers of Various Ethnic Backgrounds," presented at the National Conference on Social Welfare, Philadelphia, May, 1957.)

Poverty and Deprivation in the U.S.: The Plight of Two-Fifths of a Nation. Washington: Conference on Economic Progress, 1962.

Preparation of the Community for the Reception of Non-European Migrants in the United States: Report of the New York Working Party. Geneva: Sixth International Conference of Non-Governmental Organizations Interested in Migration, August 5-9, 1957.

Public Welfare: Myth vs. Fact. New York: Citizen's Committee for Children, 1963.

Puerto Rico—1963. Hearings before the Subcommittee on Territorial and Insular Affairs. 88th Congress, First Session on . . . Bills to Establish a

Procedure for the Prompt Settlement, in a Democratic Manner, of The Political Status of Puerto Rico. Washington: U.S. Government Printing Office, 1963.

Puerto Rican Employment in New York City Hotels. New York: New York State Commission Against Discrimination, 1958.

Puerto Rican Profiles: Resource Materials for Teachers. New York: Board of Education, City of New York, 1964.

The Puerto Ricans of New York City. New York: Puerto Rico Department of Labor, 1948.

José A. Quintero, ed., *¿Quién es quien?* New York: José A. Quintero, 1964.

Report on Finances and Economy, Puerto Rico 1963. San Juan: Department of the Treasury, 1964.

Report of a Workshop on the Southern Mountaineer in Cincinnati. Cincinnati: Mayor's Friendly Relations Committee and Social Service Association of Greater Cincinnati, 1954.

Report on Farm Labor. Washington: National Advisory Committee on Farm Labor, 1959.

Jacob Riis, *How the Other Half Lives.* New York: Sagamore Press, 1957.

Elmo Roper, *The High Cost of Discrimination.* New York: National Conference of Christians and Jews, 1954.

Morris Rubin, "Student Interpreters for Newcomers," *Strengthening Democracy,* October, 1963, pp. 3, 8.

Gerhart Saenger, *Factors Influencing the Institutionalization of Mentally Retarded Individuals in New York City.* Albany: Interdepartmental Health Resources Board, 1960.

Victor Sanua, *et. al., The Vocational Rehabilitation Problems of Disabled Puerto Ricans in New York City.* New York: New York University, Bellevue Medical Center, Institute of Physical Medicine and Rehabilitation, 1957.

Erwin Schepses, "Puerto Rican Delinquent Boys in New York City," *Social Service Review,* Vol. 23, No. 1, March, 1949, pp. 51-61.

Theodore W. Schultz, "Human Wealth and Economic Growth," *The Humanist,* No. 2, 1959, pp. 71-81.

Art Sears, "Are Puerto Ricans Negro or White?" *Jet,* XXIV, No. 15, August 1, 1963, pp. 14-18.

A Self-Help Manual on Housing Problems. New York: Council of Spanish-American Organizations, 1959.

Martin Segal, *Wages in the Metropolis.* Cambridge: Harvard University Press, 1960.

Thorsten Sellin, *Culture Conflict and Crime.* New York: Social Science Research Council, 1938.

Clarence Senior, *Implications of Population Redistribution.* New York: National Association of Intergroup Relations Officials, 1957.

Clarence Senior, *Puerto Rican Migration: Spontaneous and Organized.* New York: Migration Division, Department of Labor, Commonwealth of Puerto Rico, 1957.

Clarence Senior and Douglas Manley, *A Report on Jamaican Migration to Great Britain.* Kingston, Jamaica: Government Printer, 1955.

Henry S. Shryock, Jr., *Population Mobility Within the United States.* Chicago: University of Chicago Community and Family Study Center, 1964.

Charles E. Silberman, *Crisis in Black and White.* New York: Random House, 1964.

Ozzie G. Simmons, *Social Status and Public Health.* New York: Social Science Research Council, 1958.

A Six-Month Report of the Migration Services Department, Mayor's Committee on New Residents. Chicago: Chicago Commission on Human Relations, January, 1958; April, 1959.

Barbara Miller Solomon, *Ancestors and Immigrants.* Cambridge: Harvard University Press, 1956.

Spiritual Care of Puerto Rican Migrants. New York: Archdiocese of New York, Office of the Coordinator of Spanish-American Catholic Action, 1955.

David Spitz, *Patterns of Anti-Democratic Thought.* New York: Macmillan, 1949.

Julian Steward, ed., *The People of Puerto Rico: A Study in Social Anthropology.* Urbana: University of Illinois Press, 1956. (A Social Science Research Center Study, College of Social Science, University of Puerto Rico.)

Study of Tuberculosis Control in San Antonio-Bexar County, Texas. Washington, D.C.: Federal Security Agency, 1952.

A Summary in Facts & Figures: 1. Progress in Puerto Rico; 2. Puerto Rican Migration. New York: Migration Division, Department of Labor, Commonwealth of Puerto Rico, 1963 ed.

Frank Tannenbaum, *Slave and Citizen: The Negro in the Americas.* New York: Random House Vintage Books, 1963.

"Text of Harvard Study of the Metropolitan Area," *New York Times,* June 1, 1959.

"Thank Heaven for Puerto Rico," *Life,* March 15, 1954.

Frederick P. Thieme, *The Puerto Rican Population: A Study in Human Biology*. Ann Arbor: University of Michigan Museum of Anthropology, 1959.

Brinley Thomas, *Migration and Economic Growth: A Study of Great Britain and the Atlantic Economy*. London: National Institute of Economic and Social Research, 1954.

Frederick M. Thrasher, "Are Our Criminals Foreigners?" in *Our Racial and National Minorities*. New York: Prentice-Hall, 1937.

Christopher Tietze, *et al.*, "Personality Disorder and Spatial Mobility," *American Journal of Sociology*, XLVIII, No. 1, July, 1942.

Rexford G. Tugwell, *The Art of Politics*. Garden City, N.Y.: Doubleday, 1958.

Melvin M. Tumin, ed., *Race and Intelligence: A Scientific Evaluation*. New York: ADL, 1963.

U.S. Bureau of the Census, *Population, 1960: State of Birth*. Washington: U.S. Government Printing Office, 1963.

U.S. Bureau of the Census. *Puerto Ricans in the United States, 1960*. Washington: U.S. Government Printing Office, 1963.

U.S. Bureau of the Census. *Statistical Abstract of the United States, 1963*. Washington: U.S. Government Printing Office, 1963.

U.S. Commission on Civil Rights, *1961 Report*. Washington: U.S. Government Printing Office.

U.S. Department of Labor, *Profile 90: An Analysis of Pockets of High Unemployment in New York City*. New York: Bureau of Labor Statistics, 1963.

Albert N. Votaw, "The Hillbillies Invade Chicago," *Harper's*, Vol. 216, February, 1958, pp. 64-67.

Dan Wakefield, *Island in the City: The World of Spanish Harlem*. Boston: Houghton Mifflin Co., 1959.

Abraham A. Weinberg, *Migration and Belonging: A Study of Mental Health and Personal Adjustment in Israel*. The Hague: Martinus Nijhoff, 1961.

Welcoming Newcomers to Cities. New York: National Federation of Settlements and Neighborhood Centers, 1961.

Irving Werstein, *July, 1863*. New York: Julian Messner, 1957.

What You Should Know About Taxes in Puerto Rico. San Juan: Department of the Treasury, 1964.

Where Shall We Live?: Report of the Commission on Race and Housing. Berkeley and Los Angeles: University of California Press, 1958.

William Foote Whyte, *Street Corner Society*. Chicago: University of Chicago Press, 2nd ed., 1955.

Deborah Partridge Wolfe, *Interim Report on Education and Citizenship in the Public School System of Puerto Rico*. Washington: Committee on Education and Labor, House of Representatives, 87th Congress, Second Session, August, 1962.

Marvin E. Wolfgang, *Crime and Race: Conceptions and Misconceptions.* New York: Institute of Human Relations Press, 1964.

Index